HOW TO MAKE PRO BASEBALL SCOUTS NOTICE YOU

Also by Al Goldis:

Breaking into the Big Leagues (with Rick Wolff)
How to Get Pro Scouts to Notice You (with Rick Wolff)

Also by John Wolff

Harvard Boys (with Rick Wolff)

HOW TO MAKE PRO BASEBALL SCOUTS NOTICE YOU

An Insider's Guide to Big League Scouting

Al Goldis and John Wolff

SKYHORSE PUBLISHING

Skyhorse Publishing books may be purchased in bulk at special discounts for sales promotion, corporate gifts, fund-raising, or educational purposes. Special editions can also be created to specifications. For details, contact the Special Sales Department, Skyhorse Publishing, 555 Eighth Avenue, Suite 903, New York, NY 10018 or info@skyhorsepublishing.com.

www.skyhorsepublishing.com

10 9 8 7 6 5 4 3 2 1

Library of Congress Cataloging-in-Publication Data

Goldis, Al, 1942-
How to make pro baseball scouts notice you : an insider's guide to
big league scouting / Al Goldis and John Wolff.
p. cm.
ISBN 978-1-60239-684-5
1. Baseball—Scouting—United States. I. Wolff, John. II. Title.
GV880.22.G66 2009
796.357—dc22
2009006049

Printed in Canada

I would like to dedicate this book to the memory of my late wife, Marlene Goldis, to my parents Dorothy and the late Samuel Goldis, and to my present wife Jo-Ann Harrity-Goldis. Their support, encouragement, and commitment have been a source of inspiration and motivation for my baseball coaching, scouting and administrative careers.

—Al Goldis

To John Tumminia, the scout who made my dream come true.

—John Wolff

CONTENTS

CHAPTER ONE

BEATING THE ODDS

Every young baseball player wants to be discovered and get a shot at the major leagues. And likewise, every professional scout wants to find that "diamond in the rough"—the player who everyone else misses but who turns into a superstar. Of course, the chances of that player and the scout finding each other are, in truth, somewhat slim, but this book is designed specifically to show how you can improve the odds dramatically.

Look at this way. Scouts have been a major part of the baseball scene for well over a hundred years, and the truth is, they're pretty darned good at finding ballplayers who are prospects. For example, when Dustin Pedroia was a senior in high school, the 2008 American League MVP wasn't even drafted! Not one of the thirty teams thought the 5-foot-9, 170-pound second baseman was worth taking a chance on. But by the time he was a junior at Arizona State University, Pedroia had blossomed into a veritable hitting machine, and was drafted by the Boston Red Sox in the second round. In short, the scouts found him, even though, physically, he didn't seem as though he would big enough, strong enough, or fast enough to play major league baseball.

Pedroia even admits, "I'm not the biggest guy in the world. I don't have that many tools. If you look at me and I'm walking down the street, you wouldn't think I'm a baseball player. I have to overcome everything to prove people wrong, and so far I've done that." (*New York Times*, November 19, 2008)

These days, scouts find prospects all over the world, whether it be Australia, China, Central America, South America, the Caribbean, Canada, Mexico, Japan, Korea, the Netherlands, and so on. Heck, the other day I saw where the Pittsburgh Pirates signed a couple of kids from India who each throw 90 mph!

As you read this book, keep in mind that scouts are everywhere and anywhere. The Red Sox spotted a twenty-two-year-old flamethrower named Junichi Tazawa in Japan, and rather than wait for the Japanese pro baseball teams to sign him, Boston jumped in and signed Tazawa themselves. The price tag was $7 million.

These days, thanks to video tape and laptops, scouts are able to cover more ground than ever before, which is good, because baseball has become more and more of a global sport.

From your end, if you really think you have the talent to play pro ball, you also have to understand that you have to meet the scouts halfway. That is to say, do your part to market yourself and to make it easier for them to find you. This book will not only instruct you on how scouts evaluate talent, but ideally, will also help you how to raise your profile when it comes to being a prospect.

The Draft and You

Most baseball players and their parents and coaches only hear about the first-round draft choices: those ballplayers who are tabbed as "can't miss" prospects and sign lucrative professional contracts. But one must keep in mind that these players are extremely rare. Yes, these first-rounders do often sign for millions of dollars, but parents and players are sometimes surprised to find out that players drafted just a few rounds lower than the first-rounders don't command seven-figure bonuses. And in most cases, these lower-round draft choices are offered drastically smaller bonuses. In general, the lower the draft round, the smaller the bonus. Indeed, many kids who are drafted and sign don't receive any bonus at all.

Of course, the irony regarding all of these first-round "bonus babies" is that many of them never pan out as major leaguers. In fact, an analysis of first-rounders from the last few years shows that almost half of these "can't-miss" prospects do, in fact, miss: they never develop into major league stars, or even regular players at the big league level.

Our point is that the art of scouting is just that—an art-form. It's not a science. There are so many intangibles in judging a player's ability and predicting his physical and mental development that scouting can appear to be little more than an elaborate guessing game.

Yet each year, the June first-year player draft comes and goes. And each year for 700 to 800 hopeful ballplayers, the opportunity to play professional baseball comes true. For the thousands of other players not chosen by a club, there seems to be no recourse but to give up hope. That hope, though, is the first ingredient in pursuing any life dream. Mix it with hard work, determination, talent, and a pinch of good luck, and you may be on your way to signing that pro contract. This book is aimed primarily at the ballplayer who hasn't been drafted but still hopes to play pro ball—you're the individual we're trying to reach.

The purpose of this book, then, is twofold: one, to give you an inside look at just what scouts are really looking for in their search for professional ballplayers; and two, to help you market and sell yourself so that scouts know you exist and see you put your best skills on display. This book is written with the intent of helping you keep your dream of playing pro ball alive and flourishing. All any ballplayer wants is a shot at playing pro ball. We hope that by the time you finish reading this book, you'll be that much closer to having your dream come true.

But I Wasn't Drafted . . .

There are three ways to become a professional baseball player. The first, and admittedly the ideal route, is to be selected in the June first-year player draft that the major league teams hold each spring. The second route is to be spotted and signed as an undrafted free agent; that is, as a ballplayer who for some reason was bypassed by the draft and is approached and signed to a contract by a particular scout for a particular team. Being signed as an undrafted free agent happens more often than you might think.

The third route is to get signed by an independent professional baseball team. Independent professional baseball teams are not affiliated with any major-league organization, but rather these teams compete in independent leagues across the country. They range in talent level and have different age and playing experience restrictions based on the mission of the individual league.

For example, the Frontier League, which is a well-established indy league, focuses on cultivating young talent and does not allow players above the age of twenty-seven to compete. The Frontier League is a great place to start your career in professional baseball if you were not drafted. At the other end of the independent spectrum is the Atlantic League, which has been a popular choice for former major leaguers looking to continue their careers. As you could imagine, the level of play between the two leagues can vary significantly. There are plenty of other independent leagues that fall somewhere in between the Frontier League and the Atlantic League based upon a player's experience. Here is a partial list of the current independent leagues (new indy leagues pop up all the time) and their websites:

Frontier League—www.frontierleague.com
Atlantic League—www.atlanticleague.com
Can-Am League—www.canamleague.com
Northern League—www.northernleague.com
Golden League—www.goldenbaseball.com

Continental League—www.cblproball.com
American Association—www.americanassociationbaseball.com
United League—www.unitedleague.org

Keep in mind that in the long run, it truly makes no difference to a major league organization whether you were signed via the draft or as a free agent. Once you are assigned to an affiliated minor league club, all you will be judged on is your ability and potential as a major league prospect. No manager or coach will ask, or even care, whether you were a drafted or an undrafted free agent. All they care about is whether you can actually play the game at the big league level.

There is, however, one important but somewhat unspoken factor that can affect you and your teammates. Money. Players who receive large signing bonuses will get plenty of playing time and numerous opportunities to show what they can do. By contrast, the players who did not sign for a lot of money will not be afforded those same luxuries. If the team did not make a financial investment in you, be prepared to impress them quickly with your skills on the field. In short, the clock is ticking on everyone, but in general, it ticks a lot faster on undrafted free agents and low draft selections.

Sure, there's usually a lot more excitement when your telephone rings on draft day and there's a representative from a major league ballclub telling you that you've been selected. But professional baseball is just that—a profession. All you should really care about is getting that shot at pro ball and, ideally, the major leagues. The bottom line is simply to become a professional ballplayer, and how you get there really makes no difference.

As noted above, you might be surprised to learn just how many undrafted ballplayers are playing today in the majors. In Figure 1-1, you'll find a sample listing of big-league players and where they were "discovered." These players were passed over in the June first-year player draft. Not one club of the thirty major league teams drafted them.

And this is just the tip of the iceberg. Remember, this is just a partial listing of those undrafted players who made it all the way to the show! There are literally hundreds of undrafted players who didn't get all the way to the big leagues, yet they certainly got a chance to play pro ball because a scout gave them a shot.

Furthermore, this is not an uncommon trend in pro ball. Undrafted players have been doing well in pro ball for years. Ask your dad or your coach about just how good some of these major leaguers were: Tom Candiotti, Andre Thornton, Frank White, Ken Oberkfell, Brian Downing, Gary Ward, Jeffrey Leonard, Larry Parrish, Rich Mahler, Bob Ojeda, Jeff Reardon, and Dan Quisenberry. All of

PLAYER	HIGH SCHOOL/COLLEGE
Bobby Bonilla	HS—Bronx, NY
Mike Bordick	Univ. of Maine
Ricky Bottalico	Central Connecticut State
Will Cunnane	HS—Clarkstown, NY
Glenn Dishman	Texas Christian Univ.
Bernard Gilkey	HS—St. Louis, MO
Craig Grebeck	Cal State Dominguez Hills
Ken Hill	North Adams State (MA)
Jeff Huson	Univ. of Wyoming
Jim Leyritz	Univ. of Kentucky
Cory Lidle	HS—West Covina, CA
Marty Malloy	Santa Fe (FL) JC
Kevin Mitchell	HS—San Diego, CA
Scott Service	HS—Cincinnati, OH
Heathcliff Slocumb	HS—Flushing, NY
Terrell Wade	HS—Rembert, SC
Paul Assenmacher	Aquinas College (MI)
Bobby Ayala	HS—Oxnard, CA
Ken Ryan	HS—Seekonk, MA
Danny Rios	Univ. of Miami
Tony Saunders	HS—Glen Burnie, MD
Jason Christiansen	Cameron College (OK)
Kevin Cash	Florida State University
Chris Coste	Concordia College (MN)
Brady Clark	University of San Diego
Roy Corcoran	Louisiana State University
Justin Christian	Auburn University
Brandon Duckworth	Cal State Fullerton
Matt DeSalvo	Marietta College

Figure 1-1

Lee Gardner	Central Michigan University
Matt Herges	Illinois State University
Jason Johnson	HS-Conner (Kentucky)
Elliot Johnson	HS-Thatcher (Arizona)
Josh Kinney	Quincy University
Kevin Millar	Lamar University
Ramon Martinez	Vernon College
Darren O'Day	University of Florida
Scott Patterson	West Virginia State University
Andy Pettitte	San Jacinto College-North
Vinnie Rottino	University of Wisconsin-La Crosse
Mike Redmond	Gonzaga University
Clay Rapada	Virginia State University
Brian Stokes	Riverside Community College

Figure 1-1 (cont.)

these players had long careers in the big leagues, and not one of them was drafted.

Recent Undrafted Major Leaguers

1) Jorge Cantu
Florida Marlins
Signed as undrafted free agent in 1998.

2) George Sherrill
Baltimore Orioles
Signed as undrafted free agent in 2004 out of independent ball.

3) Greg Dobbs
Philadelphia Phillies
Signed as undrafted free agent in 2001.

4) Heath Bell
San Diego Padres
Signed as undrafted free agent in 1998.
5) Brandon Duckworth
Kansas City Royals
Signed as undrafted free agent in 1997.

6) Chris Coste
Philadelphia Phillies
Signed as undrafted free agent in 2000 out of independent ball.

7) John Rodriguez
St. Louis Cardinals
Signed as undrafted free agent after a tryout camp in 1996.

8) Randy Ruiz
Minnesota Twins
Signed as an undrafted free agent in 1999.

What did all of these players have in common? Yep—all of them were bypassed by the June first-year player draft and signed as undrafted free agents.

Want some other big league names who weren't drafted? Go back and ask your dad or your coach about Claudell Washington, Bob Brenly, Chris James, Don Carman, Rick Schu, Bryan Harvey, Mark Portugal, and Tom Niedenfeuer.

One other point—don't think for a second that only the top draft choices get to the big leagues. When you go through some of these names, you'll find it hard to believe that they weren't first- or second-round draft choices, but that's the beauty of scouting. For example, former Yankees' star Don Mattingly was a 19th-round choice. Hall-of-Famer Ryne Sandberg was drafted in the 20th round and former All-Star Keith Hernandez was chosen in the 42nd round. Then there's Jeff Conine (58th round) . . . and future Hall of Famer Mike Piazza, who was taken in the 62nd round!

Not to mention Marcus Giles (53rd round), Eric Young (43rd round), Denny Hocking (52nd round), Jose Santiago (70th round), Brad Ausmus (48th round), Brandon Villafuerte (66th round), Jason Isringhausen (44th round), Mark Buehrle (38th round), John Smoltz (22nd round), Gabe Kapler (57th round), David Riske (56th round), and Kenny Rogers (39th round).

You get the point. But even if you have great talent, you still need inner drive, determination, psychological makeup, physical stamina and, in truth, some solid marketing savvy to make your dream of playing pro ball come true. Use this book as a blueprint for your success. First, you have to know what the scouts are looking for. Then, you have to understand just what your strengths and weaknesses as a prospect are. Finally, you have to know how to market yourself in order to gain the scouts' attention.

You've often heard it said that "baseball is a business." Well, it's still a game, that's true. But ask any pro player about getting scouted and signed and they'll quickly tell you getting that first contract to play pro ball is strictly business in every sense of the word. The good news is if you read this book carefully, you'll have a much better sense of whether your dreams can come true.

CHAPTER TWO

THE SCOUTING SYSTEM

Each of the 30 major-league clubs, as well as the Major League Scouting Bureau, has its own individual scouting system. Over the years I've worked within the scouting operations of the New York Mets, Anaheim Angels, Chicago White Sox, Chicago Cubs, and Cincinnati Reds organizations. While it's true each club has slightly different wrinkles in its outlook, the truth is most clubs have organized their scouting systems in a similar way.

It is important for you, as a prospective ballplayer, to understand the differences among various scouts. By knowing how a scouting system is set up, you'll have a clearer idea regarding your chances of getting signed. Here's a look at a typical scouting organization from the bottom up.

Associate Scouts

First is the associate scout, affectionately known as a "bird dog." These individuals—who beat the high school, college, and semi-pro bushes in hopes of flushing out potential prospects (hence the "bird dog" nickname)—are affiliated with particular major league clubs, but these scouts usually do not receive salaries. Instead they may receive commissions; that is, if they find a prospect who does sign with the club, then the scout is usually rewarded with a bonus from the front office.

Rather than making scouting an all-out occupation, these men simply attend ballgames whenever they can. When they spot a potential prospect, they get the word back to their scouting supervisors. If a scout ever approaches you while you are playing at the high school, American Legion, Babe Ruth, junior college, university, or sandlot level, he will most likely be a bird dog. He may ask you some questions about your education, school, age, and so forth. He may even ask for a schedule of your games and where you expect to be playing that summer.

If an associate scout finds a player that he likes, he'll notify the club's part-time or full-time scout in that area. Sometimes the notice will be in writing;

other times it will be verbal. The bottom line is that if a bird dog thinks you have some professional promise, he'll notify the next scouting level up.

Part-Time and Full-Time Scouts

Again, organizations differ, but by and large a part-time scout draws either a small salary or just enough to cover travel expenses. He often has another full-time job, perhaps as a teacher or coach. He usually scouts in the area where he lives. If he is tipped off by a bird dog to a prospect, he will most likely check out the player in question. If he likes what he sees, he'll give the prospect an information card like the example provided in Figures 2–1 and 2–2 to fill out.

The completed forms usually go to the ballclub's full-time area scout. In most cases, he has the authority to recommend a young man be drafted and signed to a contract. However, as you'll discover, there's a big difference between recommending a player be drafted and signed and actually seeing it happen.

You can be given a prospect card at any age, particularly if you look good in a tryout camp or happen to be an underclassman in high school. It is in no way a guarantee that you'll be drafted or signed, but it's definitely a step in the right direction.

An area scout is generally assigned to one region. In densely populated areas, there might be as many as two or three area scouts. For example, in the New York-New Jersey-Connecticut area or in California, some clubs will have a couple of full-time scouts looking for prospects. Why? Mainly because there are a lot of kids to see in a short period of time. In areas less densely populated, such as North and South Dakota or Vermont and New Hampshire, there might be just one full-time or even part-time scout.

However, it should be pointed out that as scouting budgets have grown tighter in recent years, fewer scouts are being asked to cover larger territories. That puts a tremendous strain on full-time scouts to see every possible prospect in their area, and as such, they rely even more heavily on their part-time and associate scouts. Plus, these days, scouting via computer stats has become much more in vogue.

A typical case

Let's assume you're a pretty good player and you've been playing high school ball all spring. Now you're getting ready for the summer leagues. A bird dog

Prospect Information Form

Name ______________________________ Phone __________________
Address ____
City ____________________ State _____________ Zip ____________
Father's Name ___________________ Occupation ________________
Mother's Name __________________ Occupation ________________

Has anyone in your family played professional baseball? Any close friends?

____

Has anyone in your family played from college? From what school(s)?

____

What professional baseball organizations have contacted you concerning a baseball career?

____

Have any colleges or universities offered you a full scholarship or other financial assistance?

____

What is your grade point average? ________________________________

Are you considering one school more strongly than the others? Have you signed a national letter of intent to attend any of the schools?

____

How many sports do you participate in and what individual honors have you been awarded in each? Also list your batting average, HRs or ERA, and Won-Loss record for the past two seasons.

____
____
____

Figure 2-1

Information Card

Give this card to all players you have an interest in. You will need information to complete the cross-check alert—use the card to expedite information gathering. You can place your return address and stamp on this card and have the prospect or coach forward to you by mail. If possible, get all information immediately.

- ♦ Date
- ♦ Name (first, middle, last)
- ♦ Address (street, city, state, zip code)
- ♦ Telephone (with area code)
- ♦ Position
- ♦ Date of birth (month, day, year)
- ♦ Height
- ♦ Weight
- ♦ Marital status
- ♦ Glasses or contacts?
- ♦ Bat (right, left, switch)
- ♦ Throw (right, left)
- ♦ High school/college graduation (month, day, year)
- ♦ Address of school (street, city, state, zip code, telephone)
- ♦ Plan to attend college?
- ♦ College preference
- ♦ Name of baseball coach (telephone)
- ♦ Do you play American Legion baseball? (club name)
- ♦ Other amateur club
- ♦ Have you ever been drafted by a professional club? (name)
- ♦ Parents' names
- ♦ Parents' address (street, city, state, zip code, telephone)

Figure 2–2

in your town has read about your accomplishments in the local paper and has had a chance to see you play. He liked what he saw, and he got the word back to the part-time scout.

The part-time scout came to see you play the following weekend. He liked your speed and action—meaning the ballplayer's athleticism—so he alerted the area scout. The area scout looked over his schedule of high school and summer league games and realized that he could see you play on a particular Saturday when your team plays a cross-town rival. He had heard about a possible prospect on the other team as well, and figured he could watch you play against each other.

On Saturday, you showed your stuff so well the scout came down to introduce himself after the game. He asked you a few questions and gave you a prospect card to fill out. He also told you about a tryout camp later that summer and said he'd like you to attend.

Getting on the scout's laptop

At this point, you're ready to jump up in the air, pop the corks on the champagne, and tell your family and friends that you're going to be a major leaguer! But the truth is, even though you've made it to the area scout's follow-up list, there's certainly no guarantee that you're going to be drafted and signed, much less make it to the big leagues.

Certainly being approached by a scout is some cause for celebration. After all, if the associate scout didn't like what he saw, he would not have told the part-time scout about you. And if the part-time scout didn't like what he saw, he wouldn't have recommended you to the full-time scout. And even though the area scout has taken a liking to you, this only means that he'll want to follow your progress in the months to come. If, after watching you a few more times, he still thinks you're a prospect, only then will he recommend that the regional scouting supervisor see you play for draft consideration.

By this point you would have gone through an extensive filtering process that is the essence of scouting. You've been scouted numerous times by the associate, the part-time, and full-time area scouts, who all agree that you possess some professional tools. But next you have to impress the regional scouting supervisor.

On occasion, an area scout can sign a ballplayer without the approval of the regional scouting supervisor. This usually occurs just after the June first-year player draft, when the club's front office realizes that it doesn't have enough catchers, shortstops, left-handed pitchers, or whatever to fill out their Class A or Rookie League team. When that kind of shortage occurs, the word goes out to the various area scouts to be on the lookout for any youngster who plays the needed position but was bypassed in the draft.

The area scouts then go over their lists of kids who were impressive, but for some reason were not drafted. If a scout has a youngster he thinks is suitable, he notifies the front office. The front office normally gives its permission for the scout to sign the prospect and even give him a token bonus of perhaps $500 or $1,000. The youngster who gets signed by this route is usually a rugged, determined young man who makes the very most of his opportunity to play pro ball.

The Regional Scouting Supervisor's Analysis

If an area scout likes you as a prospect, he'll recommend you as a possible draft selection for his major league club. At this point, sometime before the June draft, the regional scouting supervisor will come to see you play as well. This scout oversees the various area scouts in one section of the country, and he has the perspective to judge and compare ballplayers throughout his assigned region.

But another strong word of caution. Don't ever assume that just because a scout has told you that you're going to be drafted that it's a lock. The baseball world is filled with disappointing stories of players who had been told they would be drafted, only never to get a phone call on draft day or hear their name announced during the rounds of drafting that are broadcast on the internet. This can occur because the scouting director may, at the last second, decide that he needs more pitching for the summer, and you're a first baseman. Again, this is not a reflection on your abilities—it has everything to do with what the organization sees as its immediate needs.

A definite "first-rounder"

Let's take our fantasy—your fantasy—one step further. Suppose the regional scouting supervisor also thinks you're a dynamite prospect. In his reports, he pushes you as a top draft choice, possibly even a first-round pick. You may even get an impressive final draft recommendation like the one in Figure 2–3 (see Chapter Four for an explanation of the numbers used).

Once the front office learns this, the big boss—the scouting director—will dispatch his national cross-checker to look you over. In this highly selective system, the cross-checker is one more way of making certain the other scouts

Draft Recommendation

Type prospect: *Above average*
Grade: 54
Name: ______________________
Address: ______________________
Team name: ______________________
Height: *6'0"* Weight: *190 lbs.* Age: *18* Grade: *Sr*
Bats: *R* Throws: *R* Position: *RF*
Preference Pick: *8th Round*

Position player		**Pitcher**	
Hit:	30/50	Fastball	______
Power:	50/60	Curve	______
Speed:	40/40	Slider	______
Arm:	60/60	Change	______
Field:	40/60	Other pitch	______
Base running:	40/40	Control	______
Bat speed:	60	Arm action	______
Contact:	40	Delivery	______
Make-up:	50	Make-up	______

Type hitter: Line drive, average power

Medical problems: Sprained right ankle last year while playing basketball—OK now.

Signability: Has scholarship offers at two top colleges (South Carolina; Georgia Tech) and the GPA to choose either, but he wants to be a ML ballplayer. Has cousin who plays in minors and uncle who formerly played with several organizations. Mother is very education-oriented. Scholarship program could be key that convinces him to sign.

Other remarks: Good all-around athlete. Lots of class. I recommend $______________ range to sign.

Figure 2-3

who have seen you haven't missed something. The national cross-checker sees the best prospects from every region in the country, so when he sees you, he can compare you with the best prospects from the East, West, Midwest, and so on.

The cross-checker's report will focus on your draft ranking. For example, he may think that you're definitely the best prospect in your region, but your region only rates fourth in the nation. Sometimes the best position player in one region may not be as good a prospect as even the fifth-ranked prospect in another. Or one region may have the best prospects in every position or the best in a specific position category.

Continuing our story—the national cross-checker has seen you play and he reports to the scouting director that in his opinion, you are not only a top prospect, you're the best prospect in the country. With this kind of recommendation, you can be sure that the club's scouting director will come to see you play. He will want to see for himself just how good you are before putting your name at the top of the club's list of prospects. If you're the top national pick, chances are you will get a substantial financial bonus. Before he tells the club owner he plans to sign you and give you that bonus, though, the scouting director obviously wants to see what his money is going to buy.

A simplistic overview

As you can imagine, the scenario above was simplified in many ways, but you get the main idea. Each ballclub's scouting system is based on an intricate network of checks and double-checks. By the time a club has projected you as a top pick, at least four scouts from that club alone have seen you play many times.

But even after you have gained the approval of these experienced scouts, there is no promise of success in the major leagues. Out of a typical first round of 30 players selected—that is, the first-round draftees—only about 40 percent ever really stick on a major league roster. That means that more than half of the players picked on the first round never make it for any length of time in the big leagues. Thus, you can see that even the best scouting system is fallible and the so-called "can't-miss player" is almost never found.

Consider the case of Morgan Ensberg. He was drafted in the 61st round out of high school by the Seattle Mariners. His decision to attend the University of Southern California turned out to be a great move. He was drafted four years later in the 9th round by the Houston Astros and in 2005, earned the National League Silver Slugger batting award, was selected to the All-Star team, and became an MVP candidate.

Then there's the case of superstar Roger Clemens, who grew up in the Houston area. Clemens threw in the low 80s when he was in high school. But because he was a good-sized kid (6-foot-3, 210 pounds), the Mets drafted Clemens in the 12th round out of junior college and hoped he'd sign.

Clemens, torn between playing pro ball and going to college at the University of Texas, finally decided to play ball for famed Longhorns' coach Cliff Gustafson in Austin. For Clemens, it was the right decision. Two years later, he led the Longhorns to the 1983 NCAA College World Series title, having added another 10 mph to his fastball, and then went to the bigs where he won seven Cy Young Awards.

The Major League Scouting Bureau

In the early 1960s, major league owners began to realize that some organizations, such as the New York Yankees and Los Angeles Dodgers, had become particularly efficient at signing prospects and then keeping them employed on farm teams. Scouts tried to hide any prospects they found, in hopes of signing the best players for their own system. In those days, scouts would "babysit" their prospects and shoo away any other scouts, so they wouldn't have to get involved in bidding contests for players.

Baseball owners soon realized that a system was developing in which the better and wealthier teams were establishing dynasties of talent. The teams with less talent and less money just couldn't compete, either on the field or in the pocketbook. It was a case of the rich becoming richer. To insert a sense of parity into the game, the baseball draft system as we know it today was instituted in 1965.

The concept of the annual draft was to allow the major league club with the worst record from the previous season to select first in the draft of all eligible prospects. Then the team with the second-worst record selected, and so on. In this manner, the owners were attempting to return a sense of equality to the game, trying to see to it that no club had a long-term advantage in scouting and signing the best prospects. It was an effort to help the poor compete with the rich, or at least have a fairer chance.

Many scouts felt their talents were shortchanged as a result of the June first-year player draft. Most scouts enjoyed the challenge of finding, secluding, and eventually signing prospects their counterparts had missed. But with the draft system, scouts felt it no longer mattered whether they found a hot prospect first or last. After all, if another ballclub selected ahead of the scout's team in the next draft, then the other club could tap that prospect—and the scout who originally found the player could do nothing about it.

Yet for the most part, the first-year player draft has worked extremely well in accomplishing its original purpose. Another result has been the establishment of the Major League Scouting Bureau (MLSB). Once ballclub owners realized talented prospects would be signed, not according to the scouts who found the players, but rather by each team's place in the selection process, they decided to hire a network of scouts to comb the countryside for prospects. These MLSB scouts would evaluate youngsters just like other scouts did, but instead of filing a report with an individual ballclub, they would file their reports with the MLSB.

According to MLSB director Frank Marcos, the purpose of the bureau is to supplement each ballclub's own scouting system, not to replace it. MLSB has 34 full-time and 13 part-time scouts who cover the United States, Canada and Puerto Rico. The benefit, says Marcos, is that centralized scouting reports give major league ballclubs the best information on the greatest number of prospects. One of the MLSB's greatest contributions to the major league scouting system is prospect videos. Marcos estimates they shoot video on over 1,000 ballplayers each year in preparation for the June first-year player draft. What it all means for you is this: MLSB scouts are another set of eyes out there looking for talent, and another avenue for getting into pro ball.

Baseball executives and even scouts agree that the MLSB has been a terrific idea and that it does work. Most recently, MLSB has partnered with the Urban Youth Academy in Los Angeles and Mentoring Viable Prospects in Atlanta to host an annual showcase tournament for high-school ballplayers from around the country. Aaron Hicks, a product of the Urban Youth Academy, became their greatest success story, getting selected by the Minnesota Twins in the first round, 14th overall, of the 2008 June first-year player draft.

Despite the benefits of a nationalized scouting system, every front office in baseball has its own philosophy of what the club needs to become the world champion. Some clubs think the key is team speed. Others emphasize pitching. Still others think that a solid defense is the answer. And some clubs actually break down their requirements for winning according to position.

Most recently, some ballclubs have incorporated a mathematical approach to their scouting system, using computer analysis and statistical targeting in hopes of uncovering as-yet undiscovered gems of baseball talent. Red Sox slugger Kevin Youkilis was pursued by several ballclubs based on his on-base percentage (OBP) in college, which earned him the nickname "Euclis, Greek God of Walks."

If a ballclub wants to emphasize a particular philosophy, then it makes a concerted effort to educate its own scouts as to what it wants. But if a front office is relying strictly on the reports of the centralized Major League

Scouting Bureau, it really is flying blind. A ballclub has no way to follow up or to cross-check certain players. During the 1970s, some clubs did rely solely upon the Scouting Bureau for reports. That pattern, fortunately, has dramatically changed since then as clubs realize that their own scouts are essential to the team's success.

CHAPTER THREE

HOW SCOUTS FIND TALENT

For the professional baseball scout, finding a "diamond in the rough"—the kid who everybody else passed over that becomes a superstar—is a dream come true. Scouting stories of how guys such as Rod Carew, Ron LeFlore, and Kirk McCaskill were found and signed to pro contracts make for fascinating conversation around the batting cage or in the press box.

Let's take a look at a few of these unique scouting stories, because even in a world of baseball oddities, these remain unique.

- Rod Carew, one of baseball's all-time best hitters, was "discovered" and signed by Herb Stein of the Minnesota Twins literally in the shadows of the old Yankee Stadium. Carew, who was born in Panama but grew up in the Bronx, used to play sandlot ball in Macombs Dam Park, right next to "the house that Ruth built." Stein watched Carew, liked what he saw, and signed him—a real gem found right in the Yankees' backyard.
- Ron LeFlore was serving time in a Michigan prison when he started to play ball for recreation on the prison team. His abilities caught the eye of the warden, who got word to Billy Martin, then the manager of the Detroit Tigers. Billy actually went to see Ron play inside the prison walls. He liked LeFlore's speed, power, and desire, and after going through the necessary authorities, the Tigers signed LeFlore to a contract. Ron went on to play and star for several years with the Tigers, Expos, and White Sox.
- Some years ago, I got hot when I found Kirk McCaskill, but it took a trip to one of the coldest parts of the country to do it. McCaskill was an All-American ice hockey player at the University of Vermont, and he really wanted to play pro hockey more than baseball. But after a brief fling in the American Hockey League, Kirk realized that he had a better shot of making it in sports as a major league pitcher. With that in mind, he signed with the Angels and pitched in the bigs for 12 seasons.

These scouting tales, however, are very much exceptions to the rule. For every Rod Carew or Ron LeFlore or Kirk McCaskill who gets "discovered," there are hundreds of other prospects who are scouted in more conventional fashion. That's an important point, and one you should keep in mind as you read this chapter. Most scouts are very meticulous in mining their territory in search of that diamond in the rough.

Will the Scouts Come Out?

Most amateur ballplayers aspiring to the pro ranks assume at some point during the season, a number of scouts will come to their games, watch them, and, if impressed, come back later in the season to observe again.

Is that assumption true? Remember, in any one region of the country, there are only a handful of scouts to look for, locate, and then actually watch young prospects in action. For example, in the New York metropolitan area alone, there are over 500 high schools and more than 100 colleges and junior colleges with varsity baseball programs. All of these schools and colleges play their entire schedules in a period of less than three months.

These days, though, thanks to the advent of computerized databases, online newspapers, and search engines, some of the preliminary "legwork" can be done via a laptop. Ultimately, though, the scout has to see you in action in order to make a fair evaluation of your playing abilities.

Since the New York area is fertile ground for baseball talent, a New York scout has to run from one game to another for three months during the spring, all week and weekend long. To make matters worse, most schools play their games at the same time, usually 3:00 or 4:00 p.m.

A scout can physically only attend so many games during the course of an afternoon or even one week. As a result, even the most dedicated scout misses a lot more games than he makes each season. Even if he does make it to one of your games, he may only stay a few innings before leaving to watch another.

Well, how about the summer leagues, such as Babe Ruth, American Legion, Stan Musial, Connie Mack, and the rest? Can't scouts watch those games, too? Yes, of course they can, and they do. But again, there are hundreds of summer leagues, thousands of summer-league teams, and tens of thousands of summer-league players—and only a handful of scouts in any one region.

In the last decade or so, pro scouts have found other ways to find potential prospects. One of the most popular techniques is to attend several top high school "showcase" games around the country. In effect, these are two- or three-day tryouts where not only do top college coaches come to watch prospects, but so do the pro scouts. Showcases are held throughout the country in a variety of locations, and they tend to be limited to only top prospects. Some of the better known showcases, such as the Area Code Games, or Perfect Game, or Top 96 showcases, are definitely worth checking out online. If you are a sophomore or junior in high school, these are definitely worth trying to attend. They do cost money, though, so make sure that you do your homework ahead of time, and make sure that the showcases are well-established and legitimate.

On the college front, many scouts will go to "Scout Day" at a college baseball program. Usually held during the fall, the scouts will have a chance to come in person and evaluate the member of a particular college team. If you are looking at going to college, be sure to see if that college offers a yearly Scout Day.

Setting Up a Network of Contacts

No matter how hard they try, scouts can't watch ballgames as closely or ballplayers as often as they would like. So what do the better scouts do to ensure that they don't miss a diamond in the rough?

Many scouts tackle this problem by setting up a network of reliable contacts. At the start of practice in early spring, a scout may send a personalized form letter to the head baseball coach at each high school, college, and junior college in their area.

In this letter, like the one in Figure 3–1, which usually carries the letterhead of the particular baseball club a scout represents, he asks for the coach's assistance in listing the best professional prospects he's seen, either on his own team or a competing one.

There are spaces to list players' names, positions, ages, heights, weights, and so on. The scout also usually requests a team schedule and roster. The letter is generally sent with a self-addressed stamped envelope to make the return as easy as possible.

This system—basically a form of direct mail to coaches—is an effective way to lay a foundation for an information pipeline from the coaches that pinpoints the best players in the area. A coach is usually flattered that a major league scout knows about his school and his program and has written asking for his advice and help. In fact, many coaches post a copy of the scout's letter on the team's bulletin board for all to see. Posting the letter serves as a great motivator for the coach and team because everyone knows that the scouts may be watching them. Of course these days, email and text messaging are another way local coaches can keep scouts updated on their best players. As a player, save online stats, box scores or news articles about your games so your coach can forward them to the scout. Nothing is more convincing than having a third-party reference to back up your coach's recommendations.

This method of gathering information becomes particularly effective over a number of years, as the scout develops a feel for each coach and the strength of his recommendations. For example, some coaches write back every year with six or seven can't-miss prospects, all from his team, who turn out to have been overrated. On the other hand, there are coaches who recommend only one or two prospects each season, often from other teams. The scout, having learned how tough a critic a certain coach is, will take that coach's recommendations very seriously and make certain he sees those kids. That kind of coach gives any aspiring player on his team a big advantage in the race to the majors.

I've found this direct-mail or e-mail approach one of the best ways to learn of prospects. For example, some years ago, the left-handed pitcher Jimmy Key, who pitched for many years in the big leagues, first came to my attention when Bill Wilhelm, then the head coach at Clemson, listed him on one of these letters. Jimmy wasn't very well known at the time, but after his coach got the word out, he was well scouted and became a high draft choice.

I don't want you to think that scouts listen only to high school or college coaches. I vividly recall a phone call a few years ago from Mel Zitter, a longtime coach of various sandlot teams in Brooklyn. He was calling to tell me about a skinny ninth-grader whom he described as "the best shortstop I've ever seen." Knowing Mel's long-standing reputation as a respected coach of younger players, I made sure to go down and see this young phenomenon who hadn't yet played his first game of high school baseball.

So, at the famous Parade Grounds in Brooklyn—back in those days, it was a field with more rocks than grass—I got my first glimpse of a shy youngster named Shawon Dunston. The kid was nervous and a bit tentative, but it was obvious he had great potential: In fact, four years later, he became the number-one pick in the country, and of course, played for close to 20 years in the bigs.

Newspaper Articles

Kids often poke fun at a teammate who makes a big deal about getting his name in the local paper. But certainly everybody enjoys seeing his name in

Coach Information Request

(Scout's name and address) ______________________________
____
____
____

Dear (Coach):

Would you please forward me a copy of your schedule and roster for the coming year? The baseball season will be getting started soon, and the information I have requested will be very helpful in preparing my scouting activities.

Also, I would appreciate your recommendations of any youngsters you feel that our organization should scout for the coming season. The recommendations could be for players on your team or player you have seen on other clubs.

Recommendations

Name	*Position*	*School*	*Age*	*Wt.*	*Ht.*	*Remarks*

Coach's name: ______________________________

(Scout's signature): ______________________________

Figure 3-1

print, particularly when it reflects a success on the ball field.

From a scout's vantage point, reading local papers to see who's doing well is a major aid in finding and tracking down prospects. If a local paper does a reasonably good job of covering high school and college sports, as most local papers do, then a scout can arrive home after a long day on the road and pick up the paper to see who's doing well elsewhere.

I read all the local papers I can, and I make sure all my area scouts and bird dogs read the sports pages as well. Whether it's online or in print, good scouts are always looking for information about players. For example, I might read that Jones has pitched his third shutout in as many weeks or that Smith hit two homers in a game. I make mental or written notes to follow up on Jones and Smith later in the season.

Such information is vital for scouts. Suppose, for example, that the hypothetical Jones plays for North Central High School, and that a few weeks ago, when the scout saw North Central play, Jones didn't pitch. After reading the newspaper accounts, the scout knows he has to get back to North Central on a day when Jones is pitching.

Imagine a similar situation for Smith, the heavy hitter. Maybe when the scout saw Smith's high school team play, Smith didn't play well because he was sick or hurt. Now that the scout has read that Smith is hitting the long ball, he may think it's time to go back and see him again.

Naturally, you can't control whether local sportswriters mention you as a good player, but if you have received some coverage in the press, it's a good idea to keep these clippings in a well-organized and neat fashion. If you ever write to a major league scout about your abilities, actual newspaper articles will help to substantiate your claims.

Local Sportswriters

Local sportswriters have an important role in notifying scouts about players' abilities. If your name keeps popping up in game stories or a special feature column, the scouts will be reading about you.

A local writer is assigned to cover most high school and college games. Of course, it would be unwise for you or your parents to call up the sportswriter to brag about what a great prospect you are. But there's nothing wrong with being friendly with the sportswriter, or, if you're in college, with your school's sports information director. It would be a mistake to ask a writer or publicist directly to write about you, but the better you are known to them, the greater the chance that they will mention you. So cultivate these contacts. Also consider that if you stick in professional baseball, you'll have to develop a relationship with the media. So why not practice some positive interviewing and public relations skills now?

Tournament Play and Select Teams

Particularly during the summer, baseball scouts focus their efforts on tournaments and regional playoff games, for they know guys who are serious about baseball and want to compete against the best are likely to be there.

Thus, if you plan to play on a summer-league team, make certain before you sign up that it has a good shot at being invited to play in a tournament at the end of the season or at making the playoffs. Scouts who attend those games can see how you perform both under tournament pressure and against solid competition.

To find out about these teams in your area, talk to your contacts. Talk to the high school coaches to see which teams they recommend. Talk to college coaches. Ask the folks who run the local indoor batting facility. In other words, if you do your homework, you can quickly get a sense of the better travel or select teams in your area, who runs them, when they have tryouts, and so on.

Word-of-Mouth

As comprehensive and systematic as scouts like to think they are in finding their prospects, they often hear about players through the proverbial grapevine just like everybody else.

A scout may think he's covered an entire area of the country, and then gets a call from someone saying that he's "just seen the greatest ballplayer of all time." Although usually these grapevine prospects have been exaggerated, every so often one produces a real gem.

When I first heard about Bo Jackson, he was still a high school student in Alabama. Vince Capece, the Angels' regional scout in the South, had learned about this big, strong, fast kid through the community grapevine. Vince followed up on this word-of-mouth prospect, who turned out to be a pretty good major league player. Not all leads end with a Bo Jackson, but the occasional successes make the follow-up worthwhile.

Umpires

Many scouts make it a point to get to know the local umpires. Why? Because umps often have the most objective view on ballplayers. They are on the field, right next to the players, or behind home plate. They're right on top of the action, with the best view in the ballpark of just how much that pitcher's curve is breaking, how fast a basestealer is, or what kind of hands the shortstop really has.

Umpires usually work several ball games and see a number of teams during a week. This affords them the opportunity to see ballplayers from a variety of schools and colleges. An ump with a sharp eye thus can be a source of some fairly accurate and objective comparisons.

Umpires can also quite often provide more than just an analysis of hitting or throwing skills. Since they are right in the heat of the action, they can gain valuable insights into how individual players react under pressure and adversity. They see, for example, how a young and talented pitcher reacts if a teammate makes an error behind him, or if he thinks the home plate ump has missed a call. Umpires can get a better feel for a ballplayer's psychological makeup when a call in the field, such as stolen-base attempt, goes against him.

Knowing how a player reacts to adversity is a major key in a scout's report to the front office. Does that player shrug off the call or make a big deal out of it? Does he frequently complain to the ump during a game or go about his actions on the field in a businesslike manner? Does he seem to enjoy himself on the diamond, or does he put undue pressure on himself?

To the scout looking to sign a prospect, the ballplayer's psychological profile is just as important as his physical abilities (see Chapter Five). The scout who takes the time to build up a network of contacts with umpires can gain a few more insights into a ballplayer's abilities.

As a ballplayer, if you've become friendly with an umpire, there's nothing wrong in telling him about your aspirations. If he feels you have some professional ability, he may give you the name, telephone number, or email address of some local scouts; he might even call them himself about you. Most umpires are former ballplayers themselves and would love to help a youngster get signed, especially one who asked for their help.

If you should get the opportunity to call or email a scout, introduce yourself as a ballplayer; right away say you are contacting them at the suggestion of an umpire and give his name. Tell the scout about your professional aspirations, and let him take it from there. He will probably ask basic information about you and then talk to the umpire. Just call or email the scout once, unless he asks you to call again. Give him time to do his homework on you. It is important, too, that information like the scout's name and number be volunteered by the umpire. If he thinks he can help you, he most likely will do so when you ask.

If he can't, he will probably tell you so.

Joel Lieber is a highly regarded umpire who works college and semi-pro games in the New York area. A few summers ago, I bumped into Joel when he was umpiring a game in the Atlantic Collegiate Baseball League, a well-known summer college league on the East Coast.

While we were chatting, Joel said, "Listen, Al, there's a young right-handed pitcher you ought to see in this league. His name is Phil Venturino—he's a junior out of St. Francis College in Brooklyn." I had to confess that I hadn't heard much about the kid. Joel pressed on: "He's got an excellent fastball and a hard slider. He's the best I've seen this year in this league."

Then Ralph DiLullo, one of the best-known scouts in the MLSB, told me the same thing. That was convincing enough for me. If Joel and Ralph both liked Venturino, I knew that he was worth following.

Venturino hadn't attracted much attention during his college career due to various injuries and limited playing time. But when I saw him, I knew we had a prospect. After Venturino pitched a few times that summer, I signed him to an Angels contract (I was with the Angels organization then). In his first year of pro ball, Phil chalked up an impressive 8–3 record, with a 2.27 ERA, in the Midwest League. Those are very good numbers in any league. Phil didn't make it all the way to the big leagues, but he got his shot in pro ball—and it was an umpire who tipped off the Angels to him!

Coaches

Most coaches like to be in contact with the scouts. They like to be considered as experts and enjoy tipping off a scout about a prospect or two. Whether the baseball being played is college, junior college, high school, AAU ball, travel team, American Legion, Babe Ruth, sandlot, or semi-pro, sharp scouts listen to coaches.

A talented youngster may for some reason attend a school that doesn't have a baseball team, in which case it would be likely that all his ballplaying takes place in the summer leagues. In this type of situation, the probability that a prospect might slip by a scout is greater, that is unless the summer league coach contacts the scout and tips him off.

It's easy to see that scouts and coaches invariably cross paths. Whether at a ballgame or during the off-season at a banquet, baseball convention or other function, scouts and coaches know each other and constantly talk about players and prospects.

There's nothing wrong with asking your coach if he would recommend you to a scout. He probably would be willing if he believes that you are a prospect and are interested in a pro career.

If you feel that for some reason your own coach is not making sufficient effort to push you and help improve your baseball skills, there's nothing wrong with going to the coach of another team—especially one you've played well against—and asking for his help. This demands a bit of tact and diplomacy, but other coaches are usually glad to help you out if they truly think of you as a professional prospect.

Several years back, Bryan Harvey was one of the hardest-throwing pitchers in the majors, routinely throwing in the mid-90s. But curiously, when Bryan had played high school ball in North Carolina, somehow, the word didn't get out to the scouts about him. However, his summer league coach was impressed with him and contacted the Angels' regional scout in Carolina at that time, Alex Cosmidis. Alex saw Bryan throw and signed him on the spot to a professional contract. He went on to lead the American League in saves in 1991.

Rare? Yes. But as you'll see in the next section, getting signed on the spot, especially in a tryout camp, happens more often than you might think.

Tryout Camps

Ballplayers do occasionally, though not often, get signed out of tryout camps. And though it may seem surprising, many of these players go on to become major leaguers.

When former big league manager Art Howe was playing (and was an excellent hitter for many years with the Pittsburgh Pirates, Houston Astros, and several other big league clubs), he was originally signed out of a tryout camp. Howe had been a big football and baseball star at the University of Wyoming, but due to the cold weather of Wyoming springs, very few scouts saw him play. Upon graduation, Howe was undrafted and simply returned to his home in Pittsburgh to work as a computer programmer and played semi-pro ball for fun. He played so well that his buddies encouraged him to go to a Pirates tryout camp. He did, he impressed, and he was signed.

John Rodriguez, who played for Brandeis High School in New York City, was signed after a Yankees tryout camp. As the story goes, John grew up in the Bronx and played in a summer league until one day, his uncle heard about an open tryout at Yankee Stadium. John went down to the Stadium, did well, and was signed by a Yankees scout who was impressed. Rodriguez hasn't quite made his mark in the major leagues, but he did manage an at-bat in the 2006 World Series for St. Louis.

Ray Chang was also signed after taking part in a tryout camp. After a stellar career at little known Rockhurst College in Illinois, Chang kept making the rounds of tryout camps all over the Midwest. It was after his fourth one that the Padres took a long look and decided that Chang was worth signing to a contract.

Cory Lidle had a most unusual story. The long-time major league pitcher was originally signed as an undrafted free-agent out of high school by the Twins when he was 18. He played two years in the low minors and was released after posting nondescript stats. He then signed on with an indy team in Pocatello, Utah. He did so well there that the Milwaukee Brewers took a chance on him, signed him, and four years later he was pitching in the big leagues. If he hadn't been killed in a tragic plane crash, Cory would probably still be pitching in the majors.

Going back a number of years, I recall the case of Glenn Meyers. As a senior at Columbia University in New York, Glenn hit 12 home runs and was named to the NCAA Academic All-American team. The slugging outfielder was well known to scouts throughout the East, but he was written off as being just too slow a runner. You can't sign ballplayers these days if they don't run well. Regardless, after his great senior year, Meyers waited for the June draft and hoped for the telephone to ring. But after the draft came and went without his name being called, he began to think that maybe his dream of playing pro ball was just a dream and nothing more.

I didn't know much about Glenn, but I received reports that he was playing semi-pro ball in a summer league and was continuing his slugging ways. Finally a friend of his called and pleaded with me to look him over one last time. I was conducting a tryout session for a couple of youngsters whom I considered real prospects, and so I invited Meyers along just to see what he could do—almost to serve as a measuring stick for the other kids at the tryout.

To begin with, I had the kids run a 60-yard dash. I matched Meyers against another outfielder who was a known speedster, having stolen more than 60 bases during the previous college season. When the dash was over, Meyers had won by four or five yards, in 6.78 seconds. That's very impressive—especially for a guy who "can't run." Still a bit skeptical, we had Glenn run again. And again. Each dash showed the same kind of results—6.7 and 6.8 seconds for 60 yards.

Suddenly, Glenn Meyers moved from the "no-prospect" category to being considered a real find. We already knew from the scouting reports that he could hit for power and had a good arm. Now, with the discovery that he could run, too, we knew we wanted him. By the next morning Glenn Meyers had signed a pro contract with the Angels, packed his bags, and was on his way to his first professional game.

What was the mystery about his running speed? A little investigation turned up a simple answer. A right-handed batter, Glenn consistently took a ferocious cut at the ball. By the time he untangled himself at the plate, he had already lost valuable time going down the first-base line. With a few pointers on how to correct that problem, however, Glenn was on his way. He's a prime example of a ballplayer known by all the scouts who almost fell through the cracks.

How can you excel at a tryout camp? The trick is to be at the peak of your game—a little sharper, a little more polished, and a little bit better prepared than your competition. The players invited to the tryout are presumably among the best in the area; however, only a handful will ever be signed. Your best bet is to have an inside edge. To that end, Chapter Seven will give you an in-depth look at what you can expect at a tryout camp and what scouts are looking for in players there.

CHAPTER FOUR

HOW SCOUTS RATE PROSPECTS

For every ballplayer who sweats, toils, produces, even prays for a shot at pro ball, there are many others who never see their lifelong dream fulfilled.

Some, as they continue to play, begin to realize why the scouts pass them by. Gradually they see they just don't run well enough, or hit the ball consistently, or throw strikes with the kind of velocity that a pro pitcher needs. For such individuals, the passage of time plus the natural maturation process quietly convinces them they are not quite good enough to get to the big leagues.

However, it's the rare individual who comes to this kind of realization in his late teens or early twenties. Much more common are players with complaints like these:

- *"I just don't understand it. I hit .440 this past spring, but the scouts signed that other guy, and he hit only .230!"*
- *"They [the scouts] claim I just don't throw hard enough, but look at my stats! Why, I was all-league and all-conference this year, and even threw a no-hitter!"*
- *"One scout was interested, but when he heard that I was twenty-four, he said I was too old to sign."*
- *"Okay, I'll admit I'm not much of a fielder, but nobody can hit like I do, and what about that old baseball saying, 'As long as you can hit, you can play?' Well, give me a chance; after all, I can DH, can't I?"*

Players like these, who most likely were high school or college all-stars, seem to have legitimate gripes. How is it possible for a pro scout to pass on a player who hit .440 and pursue someone who finished the college season at .230?

The distinction is that scouts are interested in statistics . . . but only up to a point. Remember, scouts are always trying to project just how good a player will be three or four years into the future. In that regard, scouts have to act as soothsayers.

Every scout makes two distinct evaluations of a player. The first assessment considers how good a player is today. The second, and much more critical evaluation, predicts how good this player will be tomorrow. That evaluation, based almost solely on the scout's "educated experience," is the cornerstone of finding professional baseball talent.

Let's use the example of the .440 hitter versus the .230 hitter to illustrate. All other factors being equal, there is no question the .440 hitter seems to be the better player today. So, in the first evaluation, the better prospect would be the guy who hit over .400.

But with his experienced eye, the scout may realize the .440 hitter has reached his peak as a player, whereas the fellow who's hitting .230 is just scratching the surface of his athletic potential. The scout predicts the current .440 hitter will never again come close to the great season he's enjoying this year. He's at the peak of his athletic performance, and his abilities will begin to slide rather than improve.

Experienced scouts will look at the player very, very carefully. Is his body lean and clearly going to grow some more? Will he fill out in the next few years? Or does he give the appearance that he has reached his fully mature size and stature? Are his legs thin, or stocky and heavy-set? Does he have to shave every day? It may sound silly, but these little tell-tale signs can truly help the scout determine whether the player has reached his full physical size, or whether he still has more growing and developing to do.

As such, with a fully-developed hitting .440, the scout may conclude that this player is already at his peak of physical performance. In short, the scout feels that the individual is as good as he's ever going to be.

On the other hand, the scout might foresee big happenings for the youngster who is hitting only .230. Maybe the young man is just developing his upper body and shoulder strength. Maybe his timing is coming around at the plate. Or maybe he's beginning to put on some needed muscle in his arms and shoulders. Whatever the reason, the scout predicts a bright career for this player as he begins to tap his athletic potential. Based on that prediction—that second evaluation—the scout might offer that .230 hitter a contract.

Let me give you an example. Several years back, there was a tremendous power-hitting outfielder named Kevin Mitchell. He was built like a bull. But if you had seen the early scouting reports on Mitchell, you would have wondered why this kid deserved a chance at pro ball. After all, his skills were very raw; he hadn't even played high school baseball. But the scouts looked beyond his rawness and lack of stats. What they saw was a true diamond in the rough—a kid who could really become a star if he became more polished.

Sure enough, Mitchell developed quickly into becoming a star slugger, and ultimately played in the majors 13 years, capturing National League MVP honors in 1989. That's excellent scouting!

Now is all of this fair? After all, the basic rule of competitive sports is that if you work hard and produce, someday you'll be rewarded for your victories and accomplishments. And every scout would agree that the player who hit .440 is entitled to every award, honor, citation, and recognition that he can get. The scouts will point to his final statistics and say, "Look—this guy hit .440. He had a helluva year!"

But just because a ballplayer has a great year doesn't mean he's a pro prospect. Yes, he deserves praise for his great season. But that is an achievement of the past. Scouts are paid to find talented youngsters who will produce in the future.

Does that mean that a player who hits .400 in college wouldn't hit well at least in Class A ball? If Class A ball were the same as the major leagues, scouting would be much easier, because many ballplayers who hit well in college could probably hit well in Class A or Rookie League ball. But it is important to note that scouts are looking to sign future major leaguers, not just kids who can play in Class A! The question is not whether a youngster is good enough to play Class A, but whether he can someday play in the big leagues.

A Job Interview

When you play ball in front of a scout, you're really auditioning for a job, much in the same way that young actors, dancers, or musicians audition for their jobs. You've probably heard the old line that "there's a light for every broken heart on Broadway." Like Broadway, baseball is a very competitive business, and getting signed to a pro contract is not easy.

Suppose you went to a job interview at the XYZ Corporation. You leave the interview feeling as though you put your best foot forward, answered all the questions intelligently, and presented yourself well. But a week or two later, you find out that the job went to somebody else. Understandably upset, you call the executive who interviewed you. He listens to you express your disappointment and then says, "Yes, we thought you were very good, but we found somebody we thought fit into our long-range plans even better."

It is important for you to understand that playing professional baseball is just that: a profession, a job, a career. A scout is not paid by a ballclub to sign nice guys who had good seasons in high school or college; his job is to find talented young men who can make solid contributions to the ballclub's future.

That's why the scout's second evaluation—of future performance—is so important. He must decide just how good a youngster will be a few years from today. Will the player get even better, or has he already peaked?

It is not uncommon for a professional scout to draft a college ballplayer who is playing second-string, while the starter at the position, ironically, is not considered a pro prospect. In the college coach's eyes, the first-stringer is right now the better player, and the scout would likely agree with that evaluation. But in terms of long-range potential, the scout sees the second-stringer will be bigger, stronger, quicker and even smarter than the guy currently in the starting lineup. From that perspective, the scout sees the present-day second-stringer as a future professional ballplayer.

Sometimes a scout may suspect that a player is playing out of position. For example, did you know that the great closer Troy Percival was originally signed as a catcher? Or that Joe Nathan, also a terrific closer, was signed as a shortstop? Mark Mulder, the lefty pitcher, was inked as a first baseman? Craig Biggio, the future Hall of Fame infielder, was drafted as a catcher and actually played in an All-Star Game behind the plate. The great Willie Mays was originally signed as a shortstop, as was Mickey Mantle. So was current Yankee catcher Jorge Posada.

Only after the scout and his coaches in the minors see a player develop and play, day after day in the minors, can they really begin to pinpoint what their current strengths are (which got the player signed) . . . and what future strengths he may have (which will hopefully get him to the big leagues).

The 20–80 Scale

Although scouting is a subjective process, many major league clubs have adopted quantitative scales to rate players' abilities. Many clubs rate a player's talents on a scale of 20 to 80, with 20 being the lowest and 80 representing all-star ability. Keep in mind, however, that this scale is based upon major league standards; that is, the prospect is being judged on how well he would stack up against current major league competition.

This is the frame of reference scouts use to evaluate talent: How well would this player do if he were playing against big leaguers? For example, a scout might rate an outstanding high school hitter as a 30 on the scale. In the scout's estimation, this youngster would probably hit as well as a weaker hitter in the major leagues, around .230, if signed right then.

At the same time, the scout might visualize this player as having the potential to develop into a top-flight major league hitter in the future. The scout believes with a few years of maturation and development, this same youngster has a future potential of a 60 using the same scale. The scout's projection is he'd be in the .290 to .310 range, which would rank him among some of the best hitters in the major leagues.

Such a rating system is vitally important (it is described in Figure 4–1). A typical 17-year-old, while he might be an outstanding high school player, isn't ready for good Class A pitching, much less major league competition. That's why he scores so low in terms of present ability. But he may appear to have big-league star potential five or six years from now, and thus rates high marks for that second evaluation.

To clarify, let's compare again two youngsters: one who was signed, one was not. The player who went unsigned was viewed by the scouts to be a 30 now, and was projected to be no higher than a 40 in the future, despite solid past credentials. That would rank him below the average major leaguer, and therefore not a good prospect for signing. On the other hand, the youngster who was listed only as a 20 or 25 now and had lower current statistics was rated by scouts as possibly developing into a 60 in a few years. Thus, he's a better prospect and worth signing, even though right now the other kid is a better player.

Playing the Detective

What are the criteria in a scout's evaluation of a player's potential development? Most scouts consider a host of items. Here's a sample:

- Size (Will he grow some more? Are his parents tall?)
- Weight (Will he get heavier in a few years?)
- Body build (Has he filled out already?)
- Strength (Has he reached his total body strength yet?)
- Body type (Are his limbs lean and long or bulked up with muscles?)
- Running speed (Will he get any faster or slower?)
- Emotional maturity (Could he handle the rigors of pro ball?)
- Health (Does he have a history of being hurt? Is he just coming off an injury?)

Only after an extensive analysis of a young man's physical and psychological history will I make a judgment of his professional potential. In the process, I will have talked with the player's coach, friends, teammates, parents, guidance counselor, coaches from other teams, umpires who have seen him, even his

Typical Team Grading System

Standard Grading

It is vital that each person involved in player acquisition thoroughly understands the standards by which grades are assigned when evaluating a free agent player or potential draftee. This understanding will affect consistency and uniformity in reporting, which are most important to our scouting program.

It is essential to understand EXACTLY what each numerical grade and its accurate description mean. Ratings of 60-arm, or 60-fastball, or 60-speed are EXACTLY the same in Trion, Georgia, as in Los Angeles, California.

When you say a youngster has a 50-fastball in the PRESENT category and a 60-fastball for FUTURE, you are telling us that his fastball is average compared to that of an average major league pitcher. But you project him to have an above-average fastball in the future, and thereby qualify him in the same category as a major league pitcher with an above-average fastball.

The same holds true for every category of evaluation. Please keep in mind that PRESENT means now in the major leagues and FUTURE means when the player realizes his maximum potential in the major leagues.

Present and Future Grades

As you will be grading high school and college players, it is likely that your PRESENT ratings will be below the average major league standard. Numerical grades of 20, 30, 40, and an occasional 50 or 60 could very well fit into that same evaluation. Because of your ability to project a player's skills overall after he gains some experience in professional baseball, the FUTURE grads should be coming in line with those of established major league players. There should be numerical grades in the FUTURE category of 40 and 50 and, in some cases, 60 and 70. Remember that when you are looking at high school and college players, you must grade them on major league standards both for PRESENT and FUTURE.

Figure 4-1

Guidelines for Grading

There are certain guidelines that you must adhere to for us to have a productive and meaningful system. The guidelines by which we will work are these:

- We will grade all players by major league standards only. You are not to grade any player on the basis that he is the best of what you are seeing at the time.
- All players must be assigned both PRESENT and FUTURE grades.

Rating Key

Numerical Grade	*Word Description*	*Comments*
80	Outstanding	The very best. Top quality.
70–79	Very good	Below outstanding but better than above average
60–69	Above average	Below very good but better than average. Still a quality player
50–59	Average	Right in the middle. Still some value.
40–49	Below average	Player has uncertain value.
30–39	Well below average	Only a mildly interesting player.
20–29	Poor	Weakest of all prospects. Interest based only on needs.

Figure 4-1 (cont.)

girlfriend if possible—all in the pursuit of getting to know this young man and what makes him tick and, most importantly, what he'll be like in a few years.

Even after that extensive investigation, developments can take place that were impossible to predict. For example, as a high school senior pitcher in Royal Oaks, Michigan, former major league left-handed pitcher Brad Havens stood a mere 5-foot-9, but because he had a strong, lively fastball, he was scouted and signed by Nick Kamzic of the Angels. In the next few months, Havens grew another three inches, and changed from a marginal prospect to a bona fide major leaguer on the way up. He went on to pitch for several years in the show.

These descriptions may make scouting sound like detective work, and in many ways it is. A scout is looking for any clues or hints that will help him to make an accurate evaluation of a ballplayer and his potential. As a ballplayer, your job is to make yourself as presentable as possible to the scout. Show the scout your best stuff. Do what you can to impress him. Remember, you're looking to get hired as a professional baseball player!

Interpreting the 20–80 Scale

Good scouts rate all aspects of a prospect, including such basic criteria as speed, strength, size, power, hitting ability, arm strength, throwing accuracy, and control. These and other important skill factors are outlined in the next chapter.

Every major league club has its own way of rating players. I prefer the 20–80 scale. Other teams use a scale like the one shown in Figure 4–2. Whatever tool is used, the prospect is gauged according to current major league standards.

I'll use outfielder and speedster Juan Pierre of the Dodgers as an example. In the category of arm strength when throwing from the outfield, Juan is a 50, about average for a major leaguer.

In my travels as a scout, I might find a youngster who also rates a 50 in terms of his throwing strength from the outfield. Such a rating means that if you were to take that youngster and put him in centerfield alongside Juan Pierre in a big league stadium, they would have equal strength on their throws.

Finding such a prospect would, of course, be rare. Few young outfielders throw with even average major league strength. A high school senior able to throw as a 50 would most likely be considered as having a phenomenal cannon of an arm compared to his current teammates.

But scouts do rate some prospects with high scores. Consider once again Bo Jackson, the former Heisman Trophy winner and star outfielder with the Kansas City Royals. You might recall that Bo started his professional baseball career on very shaky ground, and fans were asking how in the world this guy could be considered a future major leaguer. After all, he was hitting less than his weight and striking out just about every other at bat. But if you saw Bo's ratings, you'd realize that he had been chosen based on his potential as a future player, not necessarily on what he could do right now.

Specifically, the Major League Scouting Bureau graded Jackson's potential baseball skills at 75.5 (out of 80). Anyone rated over 70 is considered to be in the superstar category. Were those ratings accurate? Well, the truth is, most scouts will tell you that if Bo hadn't seriously injured his hip playing pro

Prospect Follow Report

Rating Key
8—Outstanding
7—Very Good
6—Above average
5—Average
4—Below average
3—Well below average
2—Poor

Nonpitchers	*Present*	*Future*
Hitting ability	3	5
Power	3	5
Running speed	2	2
Base running	3	4
Arm strength	5	6
Arm accuracy	4	5
Fielding	4	5
Range	4	5
Baseball instinct	5	6
Aggressiveness	5	6
Habits	Good	
Dedication	Excellent	
Agility	Good	
Aptitude	Excellent	
Physical maturity	Good	
Emotional maturity	Good	

Figure 4-2

football, he was well on his way to fashioning perhaps a Hall of Fame career. Think back to some of the monstrous home runs Bo hit. Or the way he covered the outfield with his speed. Or the amazing throws he made from the warning track. In other words, in the case of Bo Jackson, the scouts' projected evaluations of his talent were right on the money.

CHAPTER FIVE

THE FUNDAMENTAL INGREDIENTS OF A MAJOR LEAGUE BALLPLAYER

A scout who comes to watch and evaluate a ballplayer has been trained to look beyond the player's individual game performance on that particular day. He also studies intently the various components of the player's game, including the physical and psychological factors that distinguish the abilities of one ballplayer from those of another. Having observed countless ballplayers in action, the typical scout has quite an eye for identifying skills and a background of experience from which to base his comparisons and assessments.

There are five fundamental physical tools—or what we will refer to as skills—that scouts look for when evaluating talent. As I mentioned in the previous chapter, the scout not only wants to see you perform well in the game he's watching, but he is also there to analyze your potential as a professional ballplayer. To do that, he must carefully check and conduct an inventory of your physical tools.

Scouts also analyze your "mental tools." You'll learn how important those ingredients are in a later section of this chapter, "Scouting the Intangibles." A comprehensive description of what scouts evaluate as they observe ballplayers is also included in this chapter. Read this material very carefully, as it could potentially hold the key to your establishing "prospect status" and eventually landing a professional contract.

Physical Tools

Arm strength

This is a tool often overlooked by many young ballplayers. But having a strong arm, whether from the outfield, infield, or behind the plate, is essential. A strong arm allows an infielder to play deeper and thereby have greater range. Additionally, a strong arm is needed to throw out swift baserunners. The same is true for an outfielder, who has to track balls down and fire shots to the infield to keep runners from advancing. And a catcher has to be able to get rid of the ball in a hurry to throw out potential basestealers.

Thus, if you're going to show a scout your true abilities, you must be warmed up and throw the ball with your full strength during infield/outfield practice. If you throw halfheartedly or just lob the ball a scout can only assume your arm is weak, injured, or substandard. If he comes to that conclusion, you have eliminated one category by which you could be added to his follow-up list.

Running speed

Of all a player's physical tools, running speed is the easiest to judge. A stopwatch and a 60-yard dash are all a scout needs to determine how fast (or how slow) a ballplayer is. However, if pure speed were all that mattered, plenty of track stars would make great baserunners. Scouts know that speed has to be utilized properly on the base paths to be effective and that many players rely on instinct and quickness to overcome a lack of foot speed.

Once a ballplayer is labeled slow, the label tends to stick. But some "slow" ballplayers run the base paths much faster than their speedier teammates, because they run the bases better, or know how to round a base or get a good jump off a pitcher. Again, scouts are aware of these realities. You can understand, though, that a scout would prefer to sign a player who runs well.

Can You Make Yourself Faster as You Get Older?

When Hall of Fame third baseman Wade Boggs was starting out in the minor leagues, he too was considered slow or average speed, being clocked down to first at 4.3 or 4.4 seconds from the left side of the plate. Wade worked hard to improve his running speed; he even consulted with some track coaches. The coaches agreed that Wade's running style was all wrong: He was running heel-to-toe instead of on the balls of his feet. They gave him a program to improve his style, and then he worked every day to consciously change his running method. Wade eventually sliced his running time to first from home to 4.15 seconds. That didn't make him a "burner" down the line, but it also meant he was no longer considered "slow." It made a big difference in his career.

Fielding ability

A scout looks for quick hands, soft hands, and quick feet. He will tell you that it's not enough just to be able to field a ball well. He looks for a ballplayer's ability to:

- Cover a large area of the infield and outfield (range)
- Move, or jump, on the ball before it is hit (quick feet)
- Receive the ball with little effort; smoothness and grace (soft hands)
- Move his hands quickly in fielding a bad hop (quick hands)
- Get his feet set smoothly to make the throw
- Play gracefully (Does he make a difficult play look easy?)

Some players have limited running speed, but fielding instincts that give them quickness. Good scouts see that quickness. Graig Nettles and Brooks Robinson, great defensive third basemen, were never considered fast runners, but their fielding quickness allowed them to cover all sorts of ground. Remember: Quickness is not the same as speed!

Hitting ability

When I scout a hitter, I'm looking for his ability to:

- Make contact with the ball
- Hit the ball hard
- Swing the bat quickly (bat speed)
- Hit to all fields
- Be aggressive at the plate
- Make adjustments if fooled on a pitch
- Make the ball "jump off" the bat

Jumping off the bat is an expression that reflects how hard a ball has been hit. A youngster may bat .400 by hitting lots of flares, loops, "seeing-eye" ground balls, or bunts. While there's no denying that he hit .400, there is no evidence that he hits the ball hard. A scout looks for a ballplayer who consistently hits the ball with authority; that's a telltale sign of a good professional hitter.

Hitting for power

Most baseball fans assume that hitting for power means hitting a ball 400 feet or more. Although raw home run power is a major component of power hitting, some players specialize in simply hitting hard, powerful line drives. For every home run hitter in the majors, there are plenty of guys who are there because they hit the ball powerfully. There is a definite difference. As far as your performance is concerned, work to hit the ball consistently hard, and let the scouts judge how well you hit.

Scouts like to see batters who make consistently solid contact in their at-bats. Daniel Murphy, the promising outfielder with the Mets, is a good example. If you watch him game after game, you begin to realize that if Murphy gets four at-bats a game, he's going to hit the ball hard in at least three of those at-bats. That doesn't mean he's going to hit home run after home run; rather it means that he's going to put the ball into play and make it difficult for the opposing pitcher and his defense to record an out. In short, Murph hits the ball hard . . . and powerfully . . . but not necessarily for home runs.

"Major League Ability"

When I scout a player, I analyze him according to the five physical tools that have been described. If a player has average major league ability in just two of the five categories, then he's automatically a prospect I follow up on.

"Average major league ability" means a player currently has skills as good as those of an average major leaguer. Suppose a youngster has great speed and a great throw from the outfield; we'll assume that he's good enough to be rated as a 50 in both speed and arm strength. That means he's considered as good as an average major leaguer in those two categories. That youngster deserves to be followed.

I must point out that it's rare to find a high school player who rates a 50 for current ability in any category. For example, when I first saw Darryl Strawberry play at Crenshaw High School in Los Angeles, I rated him as a 25 hitter with a potential of 70. It's tough to be rated highly by a scout, particularly when you're being compared to big leaguers. But by the same token, remember that as you develop, you'll need at least two of the five criteria to be a prospect. However, many major league players aren't rated as 50s in all categories. A quality major league infielder like David Eckstein, for example, is rated, most likely, only 25 or 30 for his power and arm strength. Yet Eckstein gets much better ratings for his hitting and defensive skills. Based on his scores in those areas, he's been able to excel in the majors for years.

My point is that you must show the scouts that you do have some ability, whether it's running speed, arm strength, or hitting power. Just show it once, and the good scout will follow up on it.

What scouts look for in pitchers

So far most of my advice for playing in front of a scout has been directed to position players—that is, infielders, outfielders, and catchers. The remaining players—pitchers—aren't allowed to do much during the pre-game workout. They may shag flies or hit grounders to the infielders or throw a little batting practice. But for the most part, pitchers can only show their stuff in a game or warming up on the sidelines before their turn in the rotation.

I'll often follow a starting pitcher to the bullpen to watch him warm up. A scout can learn quite a bit about a pitching prospect by watching him throw on the side. Specifically, the scout can see whether the pitcher has much velocity, a good breaking pitch, a smooth mechanical action, good control, and so on.

A scout can't judge a pitcher merely by the way he throws in the bullpen, but he can get a preview of what the pitcher wants to display in the game. Does his ball have any movement to it? What about his move from the stretch? Does he have a third, or strikeout, pitch?

The scout may get an idea of a pitcher's maturity and experience by seeing how he warms up. Does he stretch or do calisthenics first? Does he start throwing from a short distance or a long one? While coaching plays a vital role in helping a pitcher learn the fundamentals of warming up, from the scout's perspective it's the individual preparation for a game that is most important.

A good scout does homework on a pitcher to find out basic information such as height, weight, and age, as well as to learn about any arm injuries and the last time he pitched or played in a game. Particularly at the high school level, where the best pitcher might play another position on days that he's not pitching, this kind of information is important.

Here's a good example to illustrate: I scouted Dwight Gooden as a high school senior in Tampa and clocked him at 81 mph. That's certainly a decent speed for a high school pitcher, but it was nowhere near the kind of velocity that "Dr. K" consistently generated at the peak of his career. I wanted to find out why Dwight was throwing 10 to 15 mph less than usual. Some investigation turned up the answer: The day before I scouted him, Dwight had played third base and was involved in quite a few plays in the field, many of them testing his arm. As a result, his velocity on the mound the next day was lessened. If I hadn't asked why Dwight wasn't throwing in the 90s, I might have greatly underrated his arm strength.

When observing a prospect, a scout evaluates several key components of pitching. Some of these are obvious ingredients, some are more subtle, but the experienced scout checks to see how a pitching prospect rates on each particular aspect.

Let's take a closer look at these components:

1. ***Velocity:*** Perhaps the most obvious of all pitching components, a scout first considers the amount of force, or velocity, with which a pitcher throws the ball. A typical velocity rating scale is shown in Figure 5–1.
2. ***Movement:*** Just as important as velocity is the ball's movement. Does the pitcher's ball sink, drop, slide, fade, rise, or merely go straight? The scout is usually more interested in the pitcher whose ball shows more movement.
3. ***General Mechanics:*** Does the pitcher exhibit the expected levels of maturity, poise, rhythm and pitching technique while at work on the mound?
4. ***Delivery:*** Specifically, the scout takes into consideration the pitcher's release point. Is the pitcher's delivery over-the-top, three-quarters, side-arm or submarine style? Is it free and fluid or forced and labored? It doesn't really matter to the scout which delivery style that the pitcher prefers, except that it's important that the pitcher can deliver the ball with a fluid motion and that they can throw strikes. Scouts will study

Rating Pitching Velocity

Grades (20–80 scale)	=	MPH
80	=	98+
70–79	=	93–97
60–69	=	90–92
50–59	=	88–89
40–49	=	85–87
30–39	=	83–84
20–29	=	Below 82

Figure 5-1

the pitcher from as many angles as they can, including behind the plate, from behind the pitcher, and from the sides as well. Scouts are always looking to check on the pitcher's mechanics and whether they are sound and not liable to break down.

5. ***Arm Action:*** Is the pitcher getting the full extension on his arm when he releases the ball? Is his motion herky-jerky or fluid? In other words, does his delivery make him a prime candidate for a future arm injury?
6. ***Curveball:*** When evaluating the pitcher's curve, scouts check for rotation, sharpness, direction of break (down, across, or both), and extent of break (a few inches or closer to a foot). Can a batter easily adjust to the pitch or does the pitcher hide the pitch well during the course of his windup?
7. ***Other Pitches:*** What other pitches can the pitcher throw and control? They, of course, have to be able to throw fastballs for strikes (both four-seamers and two-seamers), but they might also feature a slider, a slurve, knuckleball, screwball, forkball, palmball, or split-finger fastball.
8. ***Change-up:*** The off-speed pitch is considered vital to success in professional baseball. If a pitcher is able to throw a change-up, the scouts want to know the accuracy and frequency of the pitch—in other words, how often can he use such a weapon effectively?
9. ***Control:*** Also vitally important for success; scouts gauge whether control allows a pitcher to pinpoint certain pitches, or if the pitcher is just learning how to find the plate.
10. ***Type:*** The scouts label pitchers as certain types. Is he a power pitcher with a blazing fastball, a finesse pitcher who hits the corners around the plate, or a deception pitcher who uses a combination of good fastball, curve, and change-up to keep hitters guessing?

A pitcher must have a sound delivery, solid basics and good arm action or must show that a minor adjustment will give him these qualities in the near future. Bad arm action and poor delivery considerably lessen the chances that a scout will see a young pitcher as a prospect with potential for improvement. Experience shows that scouts can look for improvements with breaking pitches, changes of speed, and control. Even the fastball can improve with time.

Pitchers and their arms

If a scout is watching you play and you have an arm injury or are coming off one, make certain he knows about it. Remember, a scout can pass judgment only on what he sees. If you enter a game to pitch or play, he can only assume that you're healthy. If you're not at 100 percent, ask your coach to let the scout know your condition.

Before the action begins at tryout camps, scouts always ask for kids who are slightly injured or have just thrown in a game the day before to speak up. But many kids have learned to think that complaining about injuries is not "macho." Rather than saying he pitched nine innings the day before or he has an injured elbow or a muscle spasm in his back, the typical youngster will grab the ball and head to the mound or the field.

The irony of this scenario is the youngster invariably does not have a good outing and, as a result, gets crossed off the follow-up list. That can be a double loss—for the player, who should have said he was tired or hurt, and for the scout, who can only make his judgment by what a youngster shows.

What scouts look for in catchers

Catchers have to represent a combination of strength, durability, intelligence, arm accuracy, and if possible, good hitting ability. Such combinations are rare; hence, a good catching prospect is a great find. When looking at a catching prospect, scouts check the following key components.

1. ***Arm Strength:*** First and foremost, does the catcher have a good, solid throw to second base? Is there potential for that arm strength to improve?
2. ***Release:*** Does the catcher have strong wrist action? That is, can he get rid of the ball in a hurry without winding up his entire arm?
3. ***Accuracy:*** A strong arm isn't the only ability a catcher needs. Can he throw the ball directly to second base on a straight line, time and time again without missing the mark?
4. ***Hands:*** Does the catcher have hands that gently receive the pitch, or does he fight the pitch as it comes to the plate? The "softer" the receiver, the better the prospect.
5. ***Agility:*** Is the catcher good at moving around the plate? Can he easily block balls in the dirt? Can he track down pop-ups fairly well? Is he good at getting out in front of the plate to field bunts?
6. ***Leadership:*** Does the catcher show the kind of field leadership that he needs to exhibit? Does he call the pitches, or does the coach? Can he communicate well and calm down the pitcher when things get rough? And these days, with the game becoming so international in scope, it's always an added plus when the catcher is able to communicate effectively with pitchers who might be Spanish, Japanese, Korean, or

Chinese. Again, this is all part of the on-field leadership that scouts observe and appreciate.

What scouts look for in infielders

The two most important tools an infielder can have are "quick feet" and "soft hands"—the ability to gracefully field a ground ball as though it's a thoroughly natural, unhurried event. Although many scouts feel this skill is inborn and can't really be taught, the more practice you get at fielding grounders, the better you'll become. A scout will look at the following components to find a good infielder.

1. ***Range:*** An infielder must move quickly in all directions. This includes not only going to one's right or left to make a play, but also to backpedal into the outfield as well as to charge a slow roller.
2. ***Quick Feet:*** Especially for those plays around second base on a pivot, an infielder must exhibit quick feet along with agility and athletic skill.
3. ***Arm Strength:*** Like the other defensive positions in the field, an infielder must show a strong, accurate arm.
4. ***Taking Charge:*** Infielders tend to be involved in almost every play. Scouts look for an infielder's leadership abilities to see how he "takes charge" on the field. This might include taking time to talk with the pitcher, letting the outfielders know how many outs there are, directing traffic on crucial plays, etc.
5. ***Aggressiveness:*** In line with taking charge, scouts appreciate an infielder who is aggressive in his play, who is not afraid to hang tough on a pivot play or knock down a hard-hit grounder.

What scouts look for in outfielders

Outfielders tend to be regarded by some fans as offensively oriented players, but scouts, of course, know that swinging the bat is only one part of the outfielder's job. Arm strength, defensive skills, and speed, as well as several other skills, are crucial parts of the outfielder's game.

1. ***Arm Strength:*** The strongest arm in the outfield usually belongs to the right fielder because he has to make the longest throws. But scouts want to make sure that the center fielder and left fielder have good, solid arm strength as well as accuracy and quick release.

2. ***Jump:*** When a ball is hit, a good outfielder automatically gets a "jump" on the ball; he gets into position to make the next play as the pitch makes contact with the bat. Some scouts feel that this ability, like others, is more of an instinct than a trait that can be learned, but the more one practices catching fly balls, the more one can improve.
3. ***Fielding ground balls:*** Being an outfielder doesn't exclude a player from handling grounders. The ability to cleanly pick up a ball hit to the outfield, without bobbling it, is an essential part of outfield play.
4. ***Handling the terrain:*** Can the outfielder range in all directions well? Does he know how to go back on a ball, how to use the warning track, and how to play a ball off the wall?
5. ***Steps:*** When throwing the ball into the infield, does the outfielder position himself to get the most out of his throws? Does he release the ball quickly? Does he take only a couple of steps in his release?
6. ***Speed:*** Can the outfielder use his speed in covering territory? Does he know how to cut a ball off before it gets to the gap? Does he know how to charge a sinking line drive without being "handcuffed"?

What scouts look for in baserunners

Baserunning is an art form that too many young ballplayers overlook. Speed is definitely an added bonus for running the bases, but it's hardly the only requirement. A ballplayer who possesses average speed can be an outstanding baserunner as long as he has the proper instincts on the bases.

1. ***Overall Speed:*** Speed is a terrific asset to have as a baserunner. A player who can run well should exhibit that speed whenever possible, whether hustling down the first-base line, on the bases, or in the field.
2. ***Quickness:*** Not to be confused with raw speed, quickness refers to a runner's first few steps. Some runners, even those who don't possess great speed, are particularly good at getting a quick start on the bases.
3. ***Instincts:*** Scouts like to see a runner who is daring and aggressive on the bases. That doesn't mean taking foolish risks, but rather knowing when to steal a base, how to slide, how to take an extra base on a base hit, and so on. Again, the solid baserunner can couple his speed, quickness, and instincts to make himself a threat on the bases.
4. ***Sliding Ability:*** Scouts check your mechanics of sliding, including the standard bent-leg slide, the hook slide, the evasive slide (i.e. sliding away from the base to avoid a tag, and then reaching back with the hand), and

the head-first slide. Of course, many pro coaches don't like the head-first slide due to the risk of injury, but as much as they try to discourage it to their basestealers, a lot of baserunners still use the head-first approach.

5. ***Coaching Signals:*** A baserunner, while running the bases, must have the ability to see his third base coach and to find the ball on a hit-and-run or straight steal play. Scouts don't like baserunners who run with their heads down; finding the ball while you're running is essential to becoming a professional baserunner.

What scouts look for in hitters

Scouts know that there are different kinds of hitters, such as long-distance hitters, contact, line-drive hitters, and slap hitters. As Ted Williams observed many times, hitting is the most difficult skill in all of sports. Once you've found a comfortable hitting style, stay with it and keep working on it. In the meantime, the scouts will evaluate your hitting strengths and potential.

1. ***Type of Stroke:*** Scouts first classify what kind of stroke a hitter has, whether it's short and compact, long and looping, etc. The fact that there is no perfect stroke should not discourage prospective hitters.
2. ***Faults:*** Scouts also immediately check out any flaws a hitter may have in his stroke. Those flaws include hitching, overstriding, bailing out on curves, and pulling off the ball. While these flaws can all be corrected, a scout must first be aware of them.
3. ***Type of Hitter:*** There are many kinds of hitters, as identified in the following complete checklist: aggressive (free swinger), defensive (takes a lot of pitches), power hitter (home run swinger), spray or singles hitter (short stroke), line-drive, pull-hitter, straight away, opposite field, and hitter to all fields.
4. ***Power:*** Power is not restricted to home run hitters. Scouts know that a line-drive hitter can put as much power into his stroke as a home run hitter. Scouts want to see the ball "jump" off the bat; they're not interested in weak line drives or soft fly balls. They want to see how the batter hits the ball, which is the key to judging a hitter's power.
5. ***Bunting:*** Bunting seems to be a lost art, so if a hitter can bunt for a hit or put down a good sacrifice bunt, that will impress the scouts. A left-handed hitter with good speed should possess the drag bunt as a vital part of his repertoire. Too many kids avoid working on bunting skills; make sure you don't.

But What About My Stats?

Many scouts regard statistics as in indicator not so much of professional ability, but rather of potential strengths and weaknesses. That's something that many players, and their parents, don't understand.

When I look at a ballplayer's stat sheet, I'm looking for trends and subtle indices. For example, if a prospect is supposed to be a fleet-footed second baseman, I check to see how may stolen bases he has—and just as important, how many times he got caught stealing.

I look to see whether he leads his team in triples; if he's truly that fast on the bases, he should be able to stretch a few doubles. I look at his on-base percentage: a guy with great speed has to be on base to be a positive force for his team offensively. I also check his ratio of walks to strikeouts; a player with top speed should have plenty of walks and ideally few strikeouts.

Whether a prospect hits .250 or .400 is not necessarily as important as these other stats. Of course, if a player is truly top-notch, all of his stats will most likely be glittering. But many times a scout can find a less obvious diamond in the rough simply by reading between the lines of the stat sheet.

In recent years, due to the impact of the bestselling book *Moneyball*, which featured the influence of sabermetrics on the general manager of the Oakland Athletics, Billy Beane, there's no question that more scouts have placed more emphasis on a player's statistics. I must confess that I'm from the "old school" of scouting; that is, looking at a player's stats via the Internet is just another piece of the puzzle. It really shouldn't be used as the sole criterion as to whether a player is a prospect or not. Sadly, I fear that more scouts, particularly the younger ones who grew up on the Internet, tend to use stats as a quick way to dismiss potential prospects. After all, it's much easier to write off a kid than to go out, watch him play in person several times, and get a sense of what his potential might really be.

It's important to bear in mind that popular statistics, such as on-base percentage, did not get invented just a couple of years ago. It's been around for a long, long time, and all general managers and scouting directors look at the key stats of prospects. John Schuerholz, the famed former general manager of the Atlanta Braves, writes in his autobiography that every good scout will always look at stats, but only as part of the entire scouting package. That's the key to good, quality scouting.

This is not to suggest that *Moneyball*-type scouting is going to disappear. That's just not in the cards. But as someone who aspires to play pro ball, bear in mind that your high school, summer league, junior college, or college stats are more available to scouts than ever before. As noted, that could be either a blessing or a curse for your career.

But here again, even great stats are never a guarantee that an individual will be a first-round draft choice, or a prospect at all. Former outstanding Royals relief pitcher, submariner Dan Quisenberry, had an outstanding record and ERA as a pitcher at La Verne College in California. And his record was no fluke; his senior year stats were as good as his junior year accomplishments were. However, despite his top-notch collegiate career, Quiz never threw harder than 75 mph. Though he was effective against other college players, most pro scouts didn't project Dan as a bona fide major league prospect because he just didn't throw hard enough and, being in his early 20s, he probably never would throw any harder.

As a result, Quisenberry was totally bypassed in the professional draft. Eventually, after checking around with various scouts, he finally got a shot with the Royals. He signed for a $500 bonus as a free agent, but still was not considered a real prospect until he had a few good years in the minors. Dan never did develop exceptional velocity, but his unusual delivery got the job done with great movement and deception.

My point is that statistics can provide good insight for analysis, but a scout never relies solely on a player's stat sheet in deciding whether to offer a possible contract. Understanding that should give a player more insight into who qualifies as a prospect.

Perhaps the role of statistics was summed up best by famed sportscaster Vin Scully, who wisely said, "Stats are used by baseball fans in much the same way that a drunk leans against a street lamp; it's there more for support than for enlightenment." That same analogy could be applied to the use of statistics by scouts.

Scouting the Intangibles

Of all the variables in scouting a prospect, the most difficult aspects to gauge accurately are the intangibles: a player's psychological makeup, motivation, future physical changes, and other traits that are not readily apparent. Some kids are blessed with all the physical tools to become great major leaguers, but they just don't have the burning desire to compete. On the other hand there are ballplayers who are only fringe prospects because of their limited physical abilities, but who overcome those drawbacks by squeezing the very most out of their limited potential. A couple of modern-day examples would include John McDonald with the Blue Jays and David Eckstein, now with the San

Diego Padres. Understand that both of these infielders are terrifically talented players, but neither one of them is blessed with the five major tools.

These psychological variables help make scouting challenging as well as rewarding. For every first-round, number-one, "can't-miss" pick in the nation, there's another kid who doesn't get drafted, but does everything he possibly can to get signed and then fights his way through the minors to the big leagues.

Making predictions about a ballplayer's intangibles—his desire to succeed—is the most difficult part of a scout's job. That's one reason a scout will come back to see a good player again and again, in hopes of finding out a bit more about his psyche and motivation.

If a scout is watching a youngster, and the player does well that day, both the player and the scout are happy. But the savvy scout wants to be there on the day that the prospect strikes out four times in a row or gets shelled in the first inning. Seeing how a young prospect reacts to adversity can give a scout an entirely different perspective on what makes him tick.

It's easy to smile and be cordial when things are going well. But the good scout wants to know if a prospect can react positively to bad days as well. As a player in the minor leagues, you sleep in cheap hotels, take long bus rides, eat fast food, face intense competition, and play in mediocre ballparks. Nobody is there to hold your hand or to reassure you if you have a bad day or go into a slump. You're on your own, competing and scratching your way to the top.

If a scout can see how a youngster handles himself in negative situations on the field today, he has a better idea of how that player will handle life in the minors tomorrow.

The psychological makeup of a player

Many modern-day scouts would readily say that a ballplayer's psychological makeup contributes heavily to determining what kind of prospect he'll be. A scout first has to find a player with the necessary physical tools; then he must make certain that the prospect has the right psychological tools as well.

Why is the psychological aspect so important? One reason is that nearly every player who is drafted and signed has to report to the minor leagues before he can realistically be considered for a major league roster. Scouts need to sign players who can handle the arduous lifestyle of the minors. It's one thing to be a star baseball player at the hometown high school or local junior college. But what happens when a youngster is placed in a town hundreds of miles from his family and friends? Suddenly he's on his own, and has to produce against the best pitching or hitting he's ever faced.

Some kids, even ones with great potential, just can't adjust to the minor league lifestyle, and they pack it in and try another profession. To help guard against that, most clubs have guidelines like the ones in Figure 5–2 for scouts to help newly signed players.

Other players somehow know what to expect, and they persevere against the odds. These are kids who are determined to play in the big leagues, no matter how long the bus rides or how lousy the fields. And these are the kids scouts want to sign, for they have both the physical skills and the mental toughness to make the grade in this demanding profession.

Some ballclubs actually use standardized tests to gauge a prospect's psychological profile. It really depends on each organization, but most teams now openly recognize the value of psychological testing to see how their players react to such things as authority, discipline, internal motivation, and so on. Don't be surprised if you're asked to take such a test. For the most part,

Guiding the Signed Player

Individual Player Items

A very important part of the interpersonal nature of any signing is a genuine interest that you, our scout and field representative, show in the player. Many scouts feel that their job has ended once the signing has been completed. We in the ________________ organization do not subscribe to that belief.

At this point, in addition to inspecting the numbers and conditions of the player's equipment, you should advise him about the personal belongings to bring on what may be his very first trip away from home. Make suggestions from your own experience and from recent signings. Use your involvement in professional ball to help youngsters with some of their personal needs.

Instruct the young player to carry his baseball equipment on the plane with him and that he can check his personal clothing items through to his final destination. With regard to the question of how much money to bring, our organization suggests that you advise the family that $100 in case is enough. The player should also bring a check for $100–$200 so that he can start a checking account in the town where he will be playing summer ball.

Figure 5-2

What to Bring

As a guideline you might suggest the following personal items:

- Four or five pairs of slacks/dress jeans
- A pair or two of dungarees/chino pants
- One or two pairs of shorts
- A sweater or two
- Seven or eight collared shirts
- Five or six T-shirts
- One suit or a couple of sports jackets
- Two or three ties
- Underwear (six sets)
- A pair of sneakers
- A couple pairs of shoes/sandals
- Socks (athletic and regular)
- A raincoat or slicker
- Toiletries

Player Equipment

Each scout performs an important inspection of the condition and amount of equipment that a newly signed player owns upon his reporting to begin his professional baseball career.

Our ballclub may spend thousands of dollars to scout a player and then thousands more if he is signed. Yet some players are allowed to report for their professional baseball education with equipment that is lacking in numbers and substandard in grade.

When this happens, we are guilty of poor follow-through in signing a player. We also allow ourselves to use poor public relations procedures. To eliminate these problems and, more importantly, to better serve the new player and help him get started on the right foot, the home office asks each scout to do the following with regard to equipment and to advise the player accordingly.

- ♦ Ask the player to show you every piece of equipment he has. List these items, and evaluate the condition of each piece.
- ♦ Recommend that the new player have the following equipment when he leaves home to report for his first pro assignment:
  - Two pairs of spikes (both should be broken in)
  - Two gloves (one good one; the other can be old)
  - At least four sweatshirts (weight of material to be dictated by the part of the country player is reporting to)
  - At least two athletic supporters and cups
  - A jacket (windbreaker preferably): A MUST FOR ALL PITCHERS

[Note: Many high school players use heavy basketball sweatsocks under their stockings. Discourage this as players will be issued sanitary stockings for that purpose.]

Figure 5-2 (cont.)

they're painless, but for the scout and his organization, they supply another dimension about you.

Bear in mind that these tests have no right or wrong answers. As such, you certainly can't prepare for it. Traditionally, there are multiple-choice questions and the player's answers are analyzed by a computer. The player is rated on characteristics such as mental toughness, leadership tendencies, and coachability.

While a formal psychological examination is one means of measuring a youngster's desire to play ball, another approach is observing the work ethic a player displays during pre-game activities. Does he go about his business in a serious, professional manner, or does he approach the game in a lackadaisical, careless way? Does he encourage his teammates and lead by example?

Team spirit is another important quality for a player, and scouts often casually interview a prospect's teammates to learn what kind of impression he has made on his peers. Is he popular? Well-liked? Or is he thought of as a conceited and self-centered? These are additional pieces of the puzzle that a scout has to put together to judge a prospect.

Physical changes

Though most scouts are aware that physical changes occur as a player matures, such changes are sometimes impossible to predict. For example, over the last decade or so, lots of 16- and 17-year-old prospects from Caribbean countries and South America have been inked to contracts. Clearly these kids are still in their adolescence, and it's only as they grow and develop that they put on muscle and sometimes even grow a few more inches. Again, the good scout is aware of all these factors when they size up a prospect.

So how important is one's physical image as a player? Many years ago, there was a short pudgy catcher who played in the Parade Grounds in New York City. The area was full of good players, and scouts combed the park regularly for prospects. This chubby kid was a pretty decent hitter and receiver, but because he looked so little like a professional ballplayer, the scouts never gave him much attention.

Finally, though, somebody gave him a chance in spite of his weight problem. With a few years in the minors and a strict diet, that pudgy little kid blossomed into a nine-time All-Star and the 1971 National League MVP. His name was Joe Torre.

Sometimes young players complain that scouts don't pay attention to them because they're too small. Consider long-time major leaguer Marcus Giles, who stands 5-foot-8. He wasn't drafted until the 53rd round, so clearly scouts were concerned about his relatively short stature. Eric Young is only 5-foot-9, and was also a low draftee (43rd round). But he didn't let his lack of height get in the way of reaching the bigs.

A Scout's Tip for Improving Your Skills

While there's no question that professional baseball players are blessed with certain physical skills, there's also no question that an individual ballplayer can constantly improve upon his abilities and enhance his performance on the field. To that end, the following section contains several tips on how you can improve certain parts of your game. However, these are merely offered as suggestions; you should also talk with your coaches and read other books on the particular aspects of the game, such as hitting, fielding, and pitching.

Remember, the game of baseball is just as much a mental game as it is a physical one. Thus, the more you study the skills of baseball, the better ballplayer you're going to be. Remember that most of the skills in baseball take many weeks of hard work and development before you'll experience any noticeable improvement.

1. ***Overall arm strength:*** Here is a specific exercise for improving arm strength. Play catch with a friend, starting at a distance of about 60 feet. After your arm is loose, start expanding the distance gradually. Take a few steps backward after each throw, but continue to throw hard. Don't just lob the ball; throw with some zip, and throw accurately. Keep backing up until you have doubled the distance from your friend. Go back as far as you want, although eventually you'll find a limit beyond which you have to throw the ball on a hop to get it to the other player. Throwing at longer distances will build up your arm strength as well as your accuracy. However, to keep improving and see your arm strength increase, you must do this throwing daily, every time you practice.
2. ***Pitching arm:*** A scout might give you some exercises for improving your arm or show you how to increase your arm speed. Organizations have different approaches on how to build arm strength, but most of them will teach young pitchers the proper way to do long toss in the outfield, or show them the techniques they prefer when it comes to lifting weights in the off-season or during spring training.
3. ***Catching:*** Key areas for improvement include your stance, your glove position, shifting your weight, how to block a pitch, how to handle a pop-fly, pitch selection, knowledge of hitters, and how to take charge.

4. ***Infield play:*** Scouts want complete ballplayers, so they may suggest ways to polish your infield game. These will include working on expanding your range, getting in position on ground balls, and learning cut-off positions and relays.
5. ***Outfield play:*** Outfielders must know how to cover ground, get their bodies in position for a catch-and-throw play, hit cut-off men, and play a ball in the gap and off the wall.
6. ***Base running:*** Scouts want to see if you: know how to take a lead, get a good jump on a pitcher, round a base, find the ball when running on a play, have good instincts, show aggressiveness when on the bases. The following are some specific steps you can take to improve running speed:

   Step 1: Work on your upper-body strength by doing pull-ups, push-ups and, if available, bench presses. Shoulder and back strength are essential for leg speed.
   Step 2: Work on your overall strength by engaging in a weight training program. Emphasize exercises for leg muscles—knees, hips, thighs calves. Don't overdo it.
   Step 3: When you run, start with small inclines. Gradually increase the uphill nature of the workout, like football teams do in running stadium steps.
   Step 4: Alternate a pattern of jogging with wind sprints and even some distance work to build up lung capacity. Try some all-out sprints in the middle of your workouts. Go 60 yards full blast, then jog the same distance, then sprint again.
   Step 5: Incorporate this weight and running program into your regular workouts, so you do it consistently. Irregular workouts won't help as much. Keep track of your progress, maybe by getting an observer to time specific efforts over a six-week period. Don't be afraid to ask for professional help to improve your speed.

7. ***Hitting:*** You can improve your stroke by developing more upper body strength, changing your stance, shortening your stride and stroke, improving knowledge of the strike zone, or learning how to read a pitcher. Wrist and forearm strength is an important component of good hitting ability. If you want to strengthen your wrists so that the ball jumps off the bat, squeeze a tennis ball repetitiously every day. In my experience, this is more beneficial than swinging a loaded bat daily. It takes a long time to see results—months, even years—but once you develop your wrists, you'll find much more punch in your

swing. The best time to start that development is while you're in high school.

8. ***Power:*** You can enhance your power at the plate by lifting weights to improve your body strength, selecting a different weight bat, improving your selection of pitches to swing at, being more aggressive when hitting, or changing your stance or stride.
9. ***Grip:*** A scout may have some suggestions for your grip on the ball when pitching or your grip on the bat when hitting. Generally, you want to hold a bat loosely across your fingers (not your palms). For pitchers, the way in which you grip the ball (across four seams, across two seams, or across no seams) can very much affect the flight of the thrown ball.

Evaluating Your Strengths and Weaknesses

The scout's job is to observe every player on the field, so he gathers information on each one. Most amateur teams carry at most 20 or so guys, and about 12 actually get to play in the game. So a scout has to pay attention if he's going to keep track of all the players on both teams. That's one reason why scouts like to get to the games early, so they can watch infield and outfield practice. That insures them they'll be able to see a player's defensive skills, including arm, hands, range, and athletic body motion.

Many scouts make rough notes on a form similar to the one in Figure 5–3. For a final analysis, or after seeing a player more than once, a scout would complete the form again according to the instructions in "Explanation and Formula for Grading."

Figure 5–3 can be an important tool for self-evaluation as it lists specifics of what a scout is looking for. Make copies of these forms and write your own "report card" in comparison to what the scouts are seeking. Then work on the areas where you are weakest, and exploit ones in which you excel.

Scout's Note Form Rating Key

80—Outstanding 70—Very good 60—Above average 50—Average

40—Below average 30—Well below average 20—Poor

Position Player	*Present*	*Future*	*Use rating key grades* *Show times to first and dashes*					
Hitting	_____	_____	Hitch	_____	Bat speed	_____	Contact	_____
Power	_____	_____	Pull	_____	Alley	_____	Line drive	_____
Speed	_____	_____	To first base	_____	40-yd dash	_____	60-yd dash	_____
Arm	_____	_____	Strength	_____	Accuracy	_____	Release	_____
Field	_____	_____	Range	_____	Hands	_____	Agility	_____
Base Running	_____	_____	Instincts	_____	Aggress-iveness	_____	Leads	_____

Type hitter (circle proper category) Power Line drive Slap

Player's makeup

Competitiveness	_____	Honesty	_____	Teamwork	_____
Confidence	_____	Intelligence	_____		
Dependability	_____	Poise	_____		

Pitcher	*Present*	*Future*	*Use rating key grades*			
Fastball	_____	_____	Velocity (MPH)	_____	Life	_____
Curve	_____	_____	Velocity	_____	Break	_____
Slider	_____	_____				
Change	_____	_____	Fastball	_____	Breaking pitch	_____
Other pitch	_____	_____	Type	_____	Control	_____
Control	_____	_____	Fastball	_____	Breaking ball	_____

Type pitcher (circle proper category) Power Sink/slide Finesse

Player's Makeup

Competitiveness	_____	Honesty	_____	Teamwork	_____
Confidence	_____	Intelligence	_____		
Dependability	_____	Poise	_____		

Figure 5-3

Explanation and Formula for Grading

In arriving at the total grade, only the future grades are to be used. The formula is different for the position player than for the pitcher.

For the position player, you total five boxes: hitting, power, speed, arm, and fielding. Take the total of the five boxes and divide by 5.

For the pitcher, you total at the most five boxes: fastball, curve, slider, other pitch, and control. If the pitcher only shows you a fastball and curve, then you total these two plus control for three boxes. In any case, you only divide the total by the number of boxes you graded him in, and never by any more than 5.

In completing the formula, you may either upgrade or downgrade the grade after division, by anywhere from 1 to 4 points.

Example: (Position player)

Ability	Present	Future
Hitting	33	47
Power	43	52
Speed	61	72
Arm	59	61
Field	52	69
		Total these grades only

The total of the future grades in this area is 301. Divide the total of 301 by 5. The overall grade to this point is 60.2. You may upgrade this player 3 points because of his superior makeup. Add these 3 points to the 60.2 and you get a total of 63.2.

Example: (Pitcher)

Ability	Present	Future
Fastball	37	54
Curve	39	47
Slider	44	57
Other pitch	None	
Control	45	56
		Total these grade only

Because you evaluated this pitcher in four categories, then you divide by 4. The total of the future grades in this area is 214. Divide the total of 214 by 4. The overall grade to this point is 53.5.

Because of his makeup, you may downgrade this pitcher 3 points. Subtract these 3 points from 53.5, and you get a total of 50.5.

Figure 5-3 (cont.)

CHAPTER SIX

MARKETING YOURSELF: HITS AND MYTHS

The one question asked most often by baseball fans and aspiring pro players about scouting is: Where are the best places to be scouted?

Following that query is a natural corollary: Okay, once I know where the scouts are, what can I do to make certain they notice me?

These fundamental questions can be best approached as a sort of marketing problem. Let's start with some concepts held by many young ballplayers:

- *You think you're a fairly talented player, and you would like to be scouted and signed.*
- *You think you could make it to the major leagues because you have those abilities and tools that scouts are looking for.*
- *You're eager to capture the scouts' attention now.*

But balancing out the marketing equation are factors on the negative side:

- *You're not certain whether your league or team will be scouted.*
- *Even if a scout came to watch your team play, you're not sure he'd know who you are.*
- *You're deciding which college to attend, and you've always heard that the warm-weather schools attract more scouts to their games.*

Let's attack our challenge by addressing those negative factors in the process of getting scouted and signed. In doing so, we'll also deal with some of the myths about the scouting profession.

Will My Team Be Scouted?

Myth #1: Scouts watch only the bigger high schools and colleges

We have already discussed various ways that scouts hear about and locate potential prospects. For professional scouts, that process is part of doing a thorough and comprehensive job. Thus, if you play ball for an organized club anywhere in the United States, chances are excellent that the scouts in your area know about your team and will, at some point in the season, come to a game to check out the talent. Some ballplayers, though, don't believe this.

This statement couldn't be further from the truth. All scouts recognize that no school, no matter how big or well-known, has a monopoly on talent. Scouts try to cover every school in their territory during the school year, and in the summer, follow the local summer leagues as well.

Plenty of examples prove this point. For one, ever heard of Ferrum College? It's a small Division III college where hard-throwing Billy Wagner pitched. Not only was Wagner relatively small (5-foot-9) for a pitcher, scouts had to scour the hills of Virginia to find a lefty who threw 95 mph. But they found him and the Astros drafted and signed him as a first rounder.

Chris Carpenter, a Cy Young Award winner for the Cardinals, was discovered pitching for his high school in Manchester, New Hampshire. He was also a first-round draftee. Long-time major league infielder Rob Mackowiak was not only small (5-foot-10), he also played for South Suburban College in Illinois. Yet the scouts found him, and took a chance on him in the 53rd round.

Will The Scouts Know Who I Am?

If you're in a uniform and on the field, the scout will know who you are. He may not know your name and your address, at least not initially. But if you catch his eye, he'll make a mental note to follow up on you.

You don't even have to actually play in a game. A scout attends ballgames not primarily to see which team wins or loses, but to find prospects. As noted, he may spot an intriguing player taking batting or infield practice even before the game begins. That player may not even be in the game, but if he's interested, the scout will follow up on him.

I like to play a little game with myself as I scout. Particularly if I am going to watch two teams with players that I haven't seen before, I try to get to the field at least an hour before game time. Before I pick up a scorecard or a lineup sheet, I'll observe the players go through their pre-game workouts.

I try to pick out the best prospects on the field just by their movements, actions, and pre-game behavior. So if I see a big left-handed first baseman who clouts a couple of long drives during batting practice, I make a mental note to find out his name. Or I might see a wiry little shortstop who seems to gobble up every ground ball hit in his direction. Because I like his range and graceful actions, I will get his name later, too.

The point of my little exercise is to test whether I can indeed spot the best prospects on the field before I've talked with the coaches or gone over the lineups. I play this game in order to sharpen my objectivity for spotting talent.

Scouts are constantly being bombarded by coaches and the media with reports that "this kid is great" or "this guy is a definite first-rounder." By showing up at a ballpark without knowing one player from another, I can be more objective in spotting and gauging talent.

Especially at schools that have outstanding programs, it is during the pre-game period that I may spot an impressive underclassman. If I hadn't arrived early to watch the pre-game workout, I might not have been aware of this talented sophomore or freshman, because he might not ever get into the game.

It is a reality that, in some programs, talented underclassmen have to sit on the bench and wait until the current starters leave school by signing or graduating. For these younger players, showing off their talents during pre-game activities may be vital for their careers.

Myth #2: It's better to be a second-stringer on a nationally recognized team than a starter for a lesser-known club

Though scouts do observe players in pre-game warm-ups, they always prefer to see players perform in game situations. Thus, in terms of your professional chances, it's better to be with a club and actually play than to be on a nationally-ranked team that doesn't let you play much.

This applies to both college and summer league teams. They key word is play, because ballplayers often wonder whether it's better to be the best player on a relatively weak team or a good player on a relatively good one.

You enhance your chances of being scouted numerous times if you are playing regularly for a good, solid club that has other prospects playing alongside of you in the lineup. Why? If you're on a team with other talented players who are looking to get signed, they will attract scouts to your games as well.

Bryan Lambe, the national cross-checker for the New York Mets and once a star outfielder in the Detroit Tigers' farm system, makes this important point: "If your ballclub happens to have a real blue-chip prospect on it, then you know that all the top scouts in the area are going to be on hand to watch as many games as that prospect plays. And, if you happen to be on that same club, and there just happen to be several scouts at every one of your games, well, those scouts are going to have a real good look at that prospect—and at you, too.

"In other words, the better you perform and the better you look, the more opportunity there's going to be to impress the scouts and to catch their eye—even if they really didn't come to see you in the first place."

Lambe makes an excellent point. Although you may not have much choice in what kind of high school or college team you play for, you should be able to choose your summer team. If you can hook on with—and start for—a solid summer league club with some very good players, you'll increase your chances of getting noticed by the scouts.

A few summers ago, I went to Warwick, Rhode Island, to scout an American Legion regional tournament. The best Legion teams in the New England area were competing, and I was there to watch a couple of young players who were good, but they were not really professional prospects.

During one of the games, a young outfielder named Billy Swift came in to pitch a relief stint. The youngster, who was just out of high school, obviously had a strong arm, and he showed he knew something about pitching.

I was impressed and made a note to follow up on Swift. Another observer at the game was also impressed with what he saw as well. By the time the game had ended, legendary coach John Winkin of the University of Maine had offered Swift a baseball scholarship.

The scholarship offer turned out to be a smart move for Winkin and for Swift. Billy went on to have a great career at Maine, leading the Black Bears to the NCAA World Series in Omaha. He was selected by Seattle as a first-round draft choice, and went on to pitch for many years in the show. Not too bad for a young outfielder who came in to do a little relief pitching in an American Legion game.

The story of Billy Swift gives more evidence to disprove Myth #2. Swift was a good ballplayer, though not necessarily the best, playing on a good American Legion team. When he got the chance to show what he could do on the mound, plenty of scouts and coaches were there to appreciate his abilities. But the key is that Swift got a chance to show his stuff. If he never got into the game, one would have to wonder whether the scouts would have ever noticed him.

But your choice of a college should depend on your short-term and long-range goals. If you want to attend a school to pursue a high-quality education as well as a baseball career, make your selection based on a variety of criteria, including academics, cost, and location. Make baseball an important part of your decision, but not the overriding factor. There are too many considerations beyond athletics to just choose a school based upon its baseball team.

Should I Attend a Warm-Weather College?

Myth #3: You will greatly enhance your changes of getting signed if you play ball in a warm-weather area.

The relationship between which college you attend and your chances of receiving a professional contract is the subject of another baseball fallacy. In recent years I've heard high school seniors say that if they want to seriously pursue professional baseball, they must attend a college in a warmer part of the country. While there's no question that the climate in the South and Southwest is more conducive to playing baseball, outstanding programs also exist in colder climates.

The scouts know very well that talented baseball prospects can be found in all parts of the country, and for that matter, the entire world, regardless of the climate. Part of the scouting challenge is to discover talent in those areas that might not appear to be conducive to playing baseball. In short, just because you happen to live in a cold-weather area, that shouldn't discourage you from chasing your dreams of playing pro ball. Although traditionally lots and lots of players are drafted from the South or the West Coast, there are also literally countless numbers of major league stars who grew up in cold-weather regions.

Two cold-weather pro players are Derek Jeter and Jim Thome, who hail from Michigan and Illinois, respectively. Billy Swift, as mentioned, is from Maine. In 2005, the Chicago White Sox drafted Chris Getz and Clayton Richard from the University of Michigan. Roy Halladay was a star in Colorado before getting drafted. Tom Glavine was a baseball and hockey standout from Massachusetts. Slugger Matt Stairs is from Canada, as was perennial All-Star Larry Walker, who grew up dreaming of becoming a pro hockey player.

All of these young men played ball and were scouted in the northern climates of North America, where the winters are long and the springs are frozen. Judging by their success, it would appear that playing in the North did not hurt their chances of being scouted and offered contracts.

The most important aspect of playing ball is just that—playing ball. To the scouts, it makes little difference whether you're playing in Orono, Maine, or Miami, Florida. What does matter is that you're playing. If you can combine the talent and desire to play pro ball with the opportunity to play regularly and show your skills, the scouts will notice you.

Now, all this being said, while there are dozens of players who grew up in the colder areas of the country, the vast majority of major leaguers did, in fact, spend their early years in the warmer areas. Let's face it—baseball is, and has always been, a sport to be played on a warm sunny day. But just because you grew up in Illinois or Massachusetts or Minnesota shouldn't deter you from your dreams of signing a pro contract.

A Few More Myths

Myth #4: Scouts really don't know what they're doing

Although probably every player who goes unsigned has this thought, there is likely a legitimate reason that he was never offered a contract. This is not to say that scouts don't make mistakes, but in most cases, a clear-cut reason exists when a player is not considered a prospect.

As I have tried to point out, you can be an outstanding high school or college player, with all sorts of records and accolades, and still not qualify as a bona fide professional prospect. By the same token, a particular youngster may have accomplished little during his amateur career and still be looked upon as having terrific professional potential.

Let me illustrate this point with two examples. Denny Doyle, who spent nearly a decade of distinguished service in the major leagues with a number of clubs, was a top amateur collegiate player at Morehead State in Kentucky. As a senior, he led his team and its conference in hitting and was subsequently named to several all-star teams.

But when the draft came that June, not one club took a chance on Doyle. Naturally discouraged, Denny didn't know exactly what to do. While he was trying to sort out his life's plans, he helped out for a day at a local baseball camp. While he was there, a Phillies scout asked Denny why he wasn't playing pro ball. When Denny explained that he had been bypassed in the draft, the scout gave him an impromptu workout, made a couple of calls, and then offered him a contract. He was on his way.

Contrast Denny's story with that of Cameron Drew, the first-round pick of the Houston Astros in 1985.

Cameron came out of the University of New Haven, which is well known by scouts for its baseball programs. But the 6-foot-5 outfielder originally went to New Haven as a basketball player. Then, one year, Drew thought it might be fun to try out for the baseball team. He tried out as a pitcher, but he wasn't anything special on the mound. As a result, he was cast off to the junior varsity baseball squad. Cameron, realizing that his pitching exploits hadn't exactly impressed legendary New Haven head coach Frank "Porky" Vieira, picked up a bat one afternoon and jumped into the batting cage. After Drew rocketed seven or eight shots off the house across the street, way beyond the outfield fence, it was obvious that perhaps Cameron had a future as a hitter. A year later, this previously unheralded basketball player/pitcher had a sensational spring for the University of New Haven varsity baseball team, and was "discovered" as a top pick for the Houston Astros.

Myth #5: A pitcher has to throw at least 90 mph to get signed.

This baseball myth has to do with pitching. The controversies and discussions surrounding a pitcher's velocity are often heated. The average fan seems to think that a scout won't sign an amateur pitcher unless he's another Josh Beckett. Certainly every scout would like to find the next Beckett or Roger Clemens, but scouts and baseball front office people are very aware that such talent is an exception.

Let's focus on the importance of velocity, and put it in proper perspective. Hall of Famer Tom Seaver once said that the three skills a pitcher needs to win are movement, location, and velocity. On any given day, he says you can win with two of the three. But if you have only one of the three, you'll lose.

In other words, a pitcher who has great velocity, but no control or movement, is not usually considered a prospect. But, a pitcher who doesn't have great speed but does have outstanding control and movement on the ball, is a prospect. The scouts will follow such a pitcher and sign him.

For example, consider veteran left-handed pitcher Jamie Moyer of the Phillies. Jamie's typical fastball is clocked between 80 and 85 mph—below average velocity for major league pitchers. Yet Moyer has such a great curveball and slider, plus terrific command of the location of his pitches that he continues to pitch in the majors even though he turned 46 a few weeks after pitching in his first World Series in 2008.

Then there's another guy you may have heard of: Greg Maddux. This recently retired future Hall of Famer probably couldn't break a pane of glass with his best fastball, but Maddux knew how to pitch in every meaning of the word. He's shown, over and over again, that it's about changing speeds and location.

So don't be too discouraged if you can't throw a fastball like Nolan Ryan's. As one veteran scouting director says, "We're all victims of the hard throwers in the major leagues. They catch our eyes, and we'd all like to have one. But there are a lot of guys in the big leagues who throw less-than-85-mph fastballs, especially left-handers."

Another scouting colleague says, "If a young man has an average major league fastball, but it has good life, if it sinks, if he has good location, we'll take a guy like that any day."

I do want to point out, however, that it is true that scouts are attracted to guys who are blessed with golden arms who can throw a ball 90 mph or faster. When you watch television and see that the radar gun clocks the pitcher at throwing 90 plus, that's for real. And indeed, most pro pitchers do throw hard, much harder than college or high school pitchers.

But what the scouts are really looking for is that kid who is blessed with a golden arm who can also mix in his change-up, curve, and slider. When a scout finds a kid with that kind of talent, he's looking at a real prospect.

What to Do to Impress the Scouts

Dress like a ballplayer

You've heard the importance of first impressions. Well, they are important in baseball, too. If you want to be seriously considered as a prospect, always look the part.

Keep your uniform clean; if possible, wash it after every game. Don't "doctor" or customize your uniform by cutting the stirrups or rolling up the sleeves. Stand out on the field through your play, not your attire.

Does this seem silly? Well, would you go to a job interview dressed in a T-shirt and shorts? Or would you wear an appropriate business suit instead? The same philosophy applies to baseball.

Many times I look at a kid as a possible prospect just because he "looks like a ballplayer." What I mean by that is he dresses and carries himself in the way a professional ballplayer would. Therefore, he's made a positive impression before I've even seen him throw a ball or swing a bat. Just by his general manner he's caught my eye, and I'll be asking the coach about him and his talent.

Hustle on the field

Scouts go by impressions, and you can control the impressions you make. Showing that you enjoy playing ball by hustling all the time may turn the tide in your favor.

If you were a scout looking at two ballplayers of equal ability, would you be more likely to pursue the youngster who runs to his position on the field and hustles down the baseline or the player who loafs on the field and rarely runs at full speed? That's what scouts mean by hustling—they want to see just how hungry you are to make it.

Be a team player

What would you do in the following situation? The score is tied late in the game, and the leadoff man for your club strokes a double. He's the potential go-ahead run, waiting on second base. You're now at bat, with no outs.

You're a good hitter, and you ask yourself, should I swing away and try for the game-winning hit, or should I try to move the runner along by hitting a grounder to the right side of the infield? Well, as far as the scouts are concerned, the answer is simple. As a team player, you want to move the runner along to third base. That team spirit is what scouts are looking for.

What happens if you decide to swing away, and you get a base hit to win the game? You'll be happy, and celebrate, and probably read about your hit in the paper. But the scouts will know that you were selfish and gambled for a hit when instead you should have sacrificed your at-bat for the good of the team.

Subtle incidents like this occur in the course of a game or season that indicate your team spirit or the lack thereof. If you're a pitcher, a scout will notice if you become upset when a teammate makes a costly error behind you. And he will note if you openly root for teammates when they're up at bat.

Display a sense of sportsmanship

It is difficult for a scout to recommend any ballplayer—no matter how great his talent—who instigates a fight on the field or attempts to injure an opponent. That includes such actions as throwing a pitch at a batter, faking a tag so that a runner has to slide at the last moment, or sliding into a base with your spikes high. Tactics like these may seem to you the mark of a "hard-nosed" ballplayer, but as far as scouts are concerned, they label you as a troublemaker. And troublemakers don't get signed.

Be honest and forthright

If you're fortunate enough to have a professional scout approach you, don't be smug or arrogant. Answer his questions directly, politely, and honestly. If there is something you don't understand, say so. Honesty is still the best policy. Remember, that the scout is trying to help advance your career and dreams.

Demonstrate your abilities

A talented kid often assumes that scouts will read about him in the local paper or hear how good he is through the grapevine. Then when a scout does come to watch his game, the ballplayer "takes it easy"—he doesn't throw at 100 percent during practice and doesn't run out balls at top speed during the game.

It is a mistake to think that a scout will be impressed enough to sign you based on second-hand information. If you want to get signed, now is the time to show it! Scouts never sign players just because of press clippings or stat sheets. If you have the tools to become a professional player, you will need to make certain that you show those skills when the scouts are there.

Smart prospects learn how and when to impress. Let's say you're a shortstop with a great arm. But you have no way of knowing whether you'll get any plays during the game. So, to demonstrate your arm strength, make certain in infield warm-ups that you fire the ball over to first with your best throws.

A catcher or outfielder who has a strong arm should certainly display it during warm-ups. Or if you are a player with great speed and you pop one up while at bat, hustle down the baseline as fast as you can so the scouts can clock your running speed. Show what you can do! That's the key to making an impression. Give the scout something to go on.

What Not to Show the Scouts

Certain attitudes and actions will, in general, turn a scout off on your suitability as a professional prospect. Scouts are evaluating not only ballplaying abilities, but also a player's professional attitude toward becoming a major leaguer. That aspect of your appearance and on-field presence cannot be overlooked.

Never act like a "hot dog"

Scouts work at what they do because they love baseball. Some do receive remuneration for their efforts, but, by and large, nobody becomes wealthy being a scout. Because of that love and lifelong admiration for baseball, scouts tend to back off when they see a youngster—particularly a talented one—appear to show off on the playing field. It might be flipping a bat high in the air, or a unique, showy way of catching a fly ball, but whatever the action, most scouts are reluctant to recommend a youngster they have come to view as a hot dog.

There certainly are ballplayers who, admittedly, were hot dogs, and still got signed and went on to the majors. But they are relatively very, very few. But why run the risk of alienating a scout by showing off?

Avoid excess in your uniform

This bit of advice is related to the show-off pitfall. Habits that include wearing a lucky chain around your neck, an earring, or having extra sweatbands on your wrists, or rolling your shirtsleeves up while on the field may be important to you. But scouts tend to be conservative individuals by nature, and they usually have little use for the ballplayer who spends excessive time on his wardrobe.

Don't get me wrong—there's nothing wrong with these sorts of ornaments. But remember, you are trying to land a job. You want to make the best impression you can. Yes, many young players see all the flash and glitz that some current major league stars show off. But remember, these are major leaguers who have already made it to the show and have proven themselves. For example, when Manny Ramirez was in the low minors with the Cleveland Indians, his hair was short, and he never sported any earrings. Those extra accoutrements became part of his look only after he established himself as a major league star.

Don't play if you're hurt or coming off an injury

There's a difference between playing when you are in pain and playing when you are actually injured. If you happen to be less than 100 percent because of an injury, you will only do a disservice to yourself and your team by insisting on playing. If you insist on taking part in the game and your normal performances is impaired, the scout—who can only go by what he sees you do on the field—will judge you by that display.

A scout will not take the time to check before every game he watches whether a player is in good shape. If you're playing in the lineup, he assumes you're ready to be evaluated.

If you're invited to a tryout camp but you are injured, try to be there anyway. That lets the scout know you have the desire, even if you can't play. Tell the scout if you're hurt. If you don't, and you perform poorly, he might write you off.

Don't disobey your coach

Scouts are careful listeners. That's why they hang around the dugouts and around the batting cages before games. They want to learn whether a potential prospect follows his coach well. For example, suppose you're taking batting practice, and your coach yells over to "take two more." The scout watches to see whether you take only two more swings or stay up there so long that the coach is forced to throw you out.

This kind of thing is important to a scout when evaluating a player's coachability. The scout has the responsibility to determine whether a youngster has the appropriate temperament to respond to coaching in the minor leagues. Having the right attitude toward taking orders and instruction is vital in any prospect.

Never "show up" an opposing player, coach, or umpire

Baseball is a game with plenty of frustration. You already know that even the best hitters fail seven out of ten times at bat. Scouts want to see how you handle adversity, because you will see a lot of it in a pro career. As they watch you, scouts will judge your professional composure, or poise as a player. An amateur ballplayer often allows his game to be destroyed by a bad play in the field, or an umpire missing a close call, or striking out with the bases loaded. He may go into a grandstand act, throwing equipment, or kicking a water cooler, exhibiting behavior that lets everyone in the ballpark know that he thinks he has been wronged.

True professionals, however, have a stronger sense of commitment and poise. They don't like making errors, or getting burned by a bad call, or striking out, but they don't make a public spectacle of it. By and large, they keep their emotions in check, realizing that as professionals, they should take setbacks in stride and be ready for the next pitch or play.

Scouts, as you might expect, are instinctively drawn to a player who carries himself with professional poise. Nobody particularly enjoys watching an immature display on the field, and no scout wants to reward such actions with a contract.

Don't be late for practice or getting onto the field

Remember that you are selling yourself. If you want the scouts to think you really enjoy playing baseball, show them all you've got during infield and outfield practice and between innings. Sprint out to your position; fire that ball around the field. So few kids do this that you'll be a standout who catches the eyes of the scouts if you do.

Don't act tired or bored

If you give the impression that you're exhausted or that you would rather be doing something else, the scouts will respond to your attitude and write you off. Why bother following a kid who doesn't obviously enjoy playing the game?

Know the rules!

I'll bet that even though you've followed the game of baseball all your life and have played it for years, you—like thousands of other ballplaying kids—have never read, or even seen, a baseball rule book. Of course you know the obvious stuff, like outs and balls and strikes. But imagine how clever you would appear if you actually studied the rule book and put some of the lesser-known rules into operation. Scouts love seeing a youngster who knows and appreciates the finer points of the game, particularly when they can refer to the rule book for an exact interpretation.

Don't approach a scout during a game or brag about yourself to a scout

There may be occasions when you shouldn't abide by these final two suggestions. But apart from those exceptions, they should be observed.

In general, if you're playing in a game that a scout is watching, refrain from directly approaching him. Scouts cannot afford to be bashful—if one wants to talk to you, he'll find you. And if a scout does speak to you, just answer his questions. Only if he asks should you volunteer your statistics and other achievements.

In a few situations it may be worth your while to ignore the cautions about interacting with scouts. One of the exceptions would be a college senior whom the scouts have not seen play much, as a result of his being injured or platooned or on the bench. Such a player might be looking at his last chance to impress the scouts while in school, and I would say that he has nothing to lose by approaching a scout.

If this is your situation, go up to the scout, introduce yourself, and politely explain why you've decided to approach him. Get right to the point: Tell him you're interested in a pro career, and explain why you think you might have slipped through the cracks.

Don't ask whether he thinks you're a pro prospect; that's a little too blunt. Keep in mind that scouts are sensitive to pressure from ballplayers and their

CHAPTER SEVEN

WHAT YOU NEED TO KNOW ABOUT TRYOUT CAMPS

Contrary to popular belief, scouts don't stage tryout camps simply for the purpose of finding prospects and signing them on the spot. It is true that every so often a ballplayer will be offered a contract based upon his showing in a tryout camp, but this situation represents a definite exception to the rule.

For the most part, a tryout camp allows a scout and his organization to take a close look at some of the better talent in a particular area. Players are usually timed in the 60-yard dash; then outfielders field and throw from the outfield, infielders throw from the infield and field some grounders, and pitchers take to the mound to throw an inning or two. All this generally takes place in the morning. In the afternoon, there is likely a game or scrimmage that gives the scouts a chance to see players' reactions and instincts in a game situation.

Since there are 30 major league organizations, you might read about 10 or 12 tryout camps over the course of a year if you live in a major urban area. Each club wants its own scouts to evaluate and judge the talent, so if you're serious about wanting to land a contract, it is worth your while to attend as many of these separate tryout camps as you can. Not only will the experience help you, but the more scouts you impress, the better your chances of being labeled a prospect.

In contrast, most of the independent leagues do, in fact, have tryouts where they sign one or two players from those who attend. If you're searching for a professional league to play in, be sure to do your homework: go online and find that league's or team's website. Invariably, they will post the dates of tryouts. Bear in mind that these usually take place in the spring, and sometimes they are held down South.

By the way, it wouldn't hurt to do a little "marketing" of your skills. That is, have your coach send an email or make a call on your behalf to the indy team that you're interested in. It's always better to have your reputation precede your arrival at a tryout.

Open Versus Closed Tryouts

There are two types of tryout camps—open and closed. *Open camps* are just that—open to anyone who views himself as a pro prospect. An organization may run as many as a dozen of these each year. It typically gets the word out by running an advertisement or placing a short note in the local newspapers, or by posting it on the major league team's website (although you may have to search a little on the website to find it), or by telling local high school and college coaches. You could also write or call a ballclub asking for a tryout, and they will notify you about any open tryout camp in your area. (See the Appendix for a complete listing of major league baseball organization addresses and websites.)

As you can imagine, an open tryout can draw literally hundreds of players, sometimes as many as 500 in one day. The camp usually starts at 9:00 a.m. and runs all day.

I once ran a tryout camp at which 99 pitchers showed up. Since I wanted each kid to pitch at least one inning in a game situation, the camp lasted early morning until dark that night. Open tryouts can mean a long day at the ballpark, with a lot of nervous players waiting around to show your stuff.

Although you no doubt dream of being offered a contract on the spot, realistically, your purpose for attending a tryout camp is to let the scouts know that you exist, that you have some professional talent, and that they should start a follow-up card on you. If you accomplish those goals, you can consider the camp a success. Most kids who attend tryout camps couldn't sign a contract anyway, because they're still in school. (There are strict rules and regulations covering who can be signed and when. See the Appendix for more detailed information on where to find this data.)

A *closed tryout camp* is by invitation only, and only select players are asked to attend. The tryout may be held at a major league stadium; others are staged at local college or high school fields. Wherever they are held, scouts try to keep news of them quiet to avoid attracting crowds or scouts from competing organizations.

Scouts usually extend invitations to closed tryout camps via a phone call, an email, or by regular mail. Such camps are normally restricted to between 12 and 30 players, and you can assume if you're invited to one that the scouts are serious about you as a potential prospect.

Normally, the scout will have seen you play several times during the season, or has seen you at an open tryout camp. The closed session is another opportunity to compare you to other top prospects. Occasionally, a scout will invite a ballplayer who's been released by another organization and still wants to play pro ball. Or it might be a player who played indy ball last season. Or he may invite a player who looked good last year but suffered a serious injury, to see whether that person can still be considered a prospect. Sometimes a local college coach recommends a senior whom he feels has been overlooked by the scouts, and that player may be invited as well.

Closed tryout camps rarely run as long as open camps simply because there are fewer players present for the scouts to observe. The activities, however, are typically the same: You can expect to be tested on your abilities to throw, run, hit and field. In fact, in the closed camp setting you're likely to get an even more extensive workout.

The Purpose of Tryout Camps

If you will be attending a tryout camp, set your sights on simply convincing the scouts that you have talent and that they should definitely follow up on you. As you might imagine, this is a golden opportunity to be seen by the people who can help make your dream come true. Remember, the scouts at tryout camps are looking for tools: speed, hitting, throwing, fielding, and power.

You'll be asked to demonstrate your baseball tools. If the scouts like what they see, they will ask you to fill out a prospect card listing important information about yourself. If you get to this step, you deserve a congratulatory pat on the back as you have impressed the scouts well enough that they want to keep a card on you. That marks a significant accomplishment and a step forward on the road to becoming a professional.

You may wonder, "How in the world can I make an impression if I'm only allowed a few throws from the outfield or ground balls in the infield?" Although it may seem like you're not getting much of a shot, remember that the scouts are very experienced in looking for the tools of a major leaguer. They're looking for basic raw athletic material.

Also, a tryout camp is not the type of setting where a scout attempts to judge your instincts, your ability to play in a game situation, or your desire to win. Rather, it is an opportunity for a scout to check out the players' basic baseball abilities.

Your primary aim in this kind of tryout is to impress the scout with your physical abilities. Don't hold anything back—give it your best shot. If the scouts like what they see, they'll return to watch you play in a regular game.

Remember, too, that at these camps you'll be surrounded by a wide variety of baseball players—skinny, nervous high schoolers who don't know what to expect, seasoned college seniors who are looking to sign, or junior college players who want scouts to notice them. You'll see kids who look terrific and kids who seem to have hardly picked up a baseball before. From the scouts' perspective, tryout camps bring together a great cross-section sample of the available talent in your area.

The Open Tryout Camp

Your first activity at camp will be to register your name, age, school, and position on a sheet provided by the scout. You'll probably be asked to sign a form, similar to the one shown in Figure 7–1, asking you to agree that you will not hold the major league club or scout responsible if you are injured during the camp. Read the sheet to know what you're signing; but understand that unless you do sign it, you won't be allowed to participate.

Release From Responsibility

The ____________________________ major league baseball club and its affiliates and employees will not be responsible or liable for any injury you may incur during or after the tryout camp.
You are attending this tryout camp at your own risk. Should you receive any type of injury, it will be your own financial responsibility. You will NOT be allowed to participate in the tryout camp unless you have signed this form (if you are under 21 years of age, your parent or legal guardian must sign). You must present this SIGNED form to our scout or tryout coordinator before entering the tryout camp.

____
Parent or Guardian

____________________________ ____________________________
Player Date

Figure 7–1

The atmosphere at the start of your tryout camp may be like a carnival or a parade: a carnival because everybody is eager to get the action going, and a parade because of all the different uniforms.

Chances are good that you'll see some buddies there. There's nothing wrong with chatting with them before the camp begins or when you're not participating. However, when the head scout speaks to the group, stop talking and pay attention. You don't want to appear disinterested or miss important instructions. Pay attention!

Bring your own equipment!

When you prepare for the tryout camp, imagine that you're going to an all-day job interview. Your uniform should be clean, pressed, and in good condition; your shoes should be shined and well broken in. Bring a jacket, especially if you're a pitcher, and a change of undershirt.

You should also bring along something light to eat, such as a sandwich and plenty to drink. Don't assume that the field will have a water fountain, a clubhouse, or a bathroom. Eat a good-sized breakfast and arrive at the ballpark fully dressed and ready to work out.

In terms of equipment, assume nothing will be provided for you. Bring your own glove (or gloves, you play different positions) and bat (aluminum is okay, although the scouts prefer that you bring wooden ones). Bring your own batting helmet, batting gloves, etc. If you're a catcher, bring along your own catching equipment. In short, a day or two before the tryout, prepare a checklist of equipment, just like a scout does. Figure 7–2 shows you what the scout brings to a tryout camp.

The action

Most open tryout camps are similar in style, but each organization goes by its own format. Look over the outline in Figure 7–3 for a behind-the-scenes look at the administration of a typical camp. You can gain an edge over the other participants by knowing beforehand what to expect and by practicing those exercises that you'll be asked to perform during the tryout.

Once the administration matters are taken care of, the ballplayers usually take a lap around the field to get loose. Do some stretching on your own and some calisthenics if you want. Because the first test in the typical camp will be a 60-yard dash, it's important to loosen up and break a sweat so that your legs are warmed up and ready to go hard. I would suggest that before your name is

Tryout Camp Equipment Needs

- Baseballs (use new balls for pitchers and infield drill, used balls for batting)
- Catching equipment, including masks, shin guards, chest protectors, etc. (two sets: game and bullpen)
- Tryout camp forms
- Tryout camp registration cards
- Tape measure for 60-yard dash
- Stopwatches (2)
- Pencils
- Clipboards (enough for all workers)
- Carbon paper (make enough copies for office and associates)

If you have a grounds crew, tip them for their time and assistance.

[NOTE: All equipment is available from the home office except for the 60-yard tape measure, clipboards, stopwatches, and pencils. Please purchase any of those items if you need them. Have plenty of pencils for registration.]

Figure 7–2

called, get loose and then run a practice 60 yards at full speed. Why? Because you will run a faster time when your legs are really loose and your body is pumping with adrenaline. Thus, if you run a practice dash, your second one—the one that counts—will show a better time.

Usually the 60-yard dash is run in the outfield, on grass. The scouts mark off the distance and then stage the timings by calling out players' names. You may run by yourself or, if there are many kids to time, you'll run against another player.

If you are running alone, the scout will start timing you when you make your first move. That is, instead of giving you a "ready . . . set . . . go," he'll start the clock as soon as you break from the mark.

Many kids wonder whether it's better to start from a sprinter's crouch or a basestealer's position, with the legs straddled. I prefer to see a ballplayer start from the base stealing position; after all, that's the kind of start you're going to get in a game. And since you're timed from your first movement, starting like a basestealer as opposed to a sprinter should make little difference in your time.

If you run against another player, the scout normally will give you a "ready . . . set . . . go" so both runners start at the same time. The readings in these races tend to be accurate for the first runner, but less so for the one who comes in second. But don't worry: if the scout wants to see you run again, he'll ask. In most tryout camps, you'll run at least two 60-yarders.

What's a good time? By and large, if you finish in 7.0 seconds or less (7.1 is considered average for a major leaguer), the scout will take careful note of your name and speed. For more detailed information on the running aspect of the tryout camp, read Figure 7–4. Take note of what the scouts look for, and key your practices to those expectations.

Outfield and infield throwing

Once the running is completed, the scouts will most likely test players' outfield and infield arms—specifically, arm strength and accuracy. Participants are divided into pairs to throw to each other and loosen their arms up.

The outfielders then are called to center field. At a mark of 250 feet from home, you'll be asked to catch a fly ball, field a grounder, and field a line drive on one hop.

The scouts will watch to see how you approach the ball, how you position your body, and how you surround the ball. They'll evaluate your arm strength on your throw to the infield. You may throw to second base or to a cutoff man on the pitcher's mound.

Scouts look for kids who get their bodies under control in the outfield; who have quick arm action and release of the ball, a coordinated throwing action, and accuracy in throwing to a certain spot; and who have great carry on the ball. By carry, I mean that the throw is strong—it doesn't fade or die away as it approaches the cutoff man.

Remember to catch the ball with two hands and grasp it across the seams. All major league outfielders hold the ball "four seams," which ensures that their throws are straight and true and do not sail off the mark. When the ball does bounce, it bounces in a straight line, not off to the side.

Once the outfield action is completed, infielders are placed at shortstop and asked to field three or four grounders and to make throws across to first base. Try to emphasize fundamentals here; keep in mind that the scouts are looking for professional actions. Get your body in front of the ball, keep your backside down, get your arms and hands out in front of your body, plant your back foot solidly, and make a good, hard, on-balance throw to first.

Show quick feet in your infield play. Scouts are looking at you from head to toe, and for infielders—particularly shortstops and second basemen—quick feet are essential. That means being able to adjust your body hurriedly in case of a bad hop or being coordinated enough to move your feet into a fielding position on a tough play.

Stay on your toes in the infield and move as fast as you can for the grounders hit your way. Never give the impression that you're plodding along or that you're heavy-footed. Look alert, look quick, and move, move, move!

Once the infielders have finished, the first baseman will be asked to field grounders and throw across the diamond to third. Scouts look for the same kind of skills here: smooth actions, soft hands, quick feet, good range, and an accurate and solid throw.

Catchers are placed behind home and asked to throw out to second base in a simulated stolen-base situation. With a stopwatch, a scout will measure your release time and arm strength (the time of the throw to second base). You'll be given only a few throws, so make certain your arm is loose and ready.

Players who play more than one position

If you have played both outfield and infield recently with your club, or if you pitch and also play another position, then by all means try out at both spots. The same goes if you're a catcher and also play another position. Be sure to give the scouts that information on the sign-up sheet. If you have played two positions but think that you're much better at one, though, try out at your better position only.

Pitchers

Most scouts have pitchers throw at least one inning in a game situation. First, though, you will throw on the sidelines while a scout observes. Here, the scout is looking for basic tools: velocity, movement, mechanics, breaking pitches, control, and general athletic ability. A scout can usually tell from this brief observation period whether a pitcher has the skills to make it as a pro even without watching the pitcher throw to a live batter.

Don't be discouraged if you aren't the hardest thrower at the camp. Although any scout would love to find a youngster with a 90-mph fastball, he knows that such pitchers are rare. If your fastball is in the 80s and you have excellent location, great movement on the ball, or an outstanding breaking pitch, a scout will certainly take note of you.

On the sidelines you will only throw 20 to 25 pitches, so don't hold back. Although you'll be tempted, don't overthrow either. Make certain you can control what you throw. You have to be able to throw strikes!

To the game!

If there is enough time after the testing is completed, the scouts will hold a quick round of infield/outfield practice. If this happens, go to the position where you feel the most comfortable.

Try to show plenty of spark. Make noise. Whistle. You're competing against all the players there to capture the scouts' attention. If you're good at making chatter, that's another way to let scouts know you're a ballplayer worth watching.

In a simulated game, two teams will be put together haphazardly, and a parade of pitchers will throw one inning (six outs) each. There is little rhyme or reason to how the teams are drawn up, so don't worry about what team you're on or where you bat in the order. In fact, the batting order may just go round the defensive lineup; that is, the catcher hits first, then the first baseman, the second baseman, and so on.

If you're not selected to play in the first lineup, find a place off the field in the shade and relax. The action often goes fairly quickly and, as each batter gets his turn (usually two at-bats), he is replaced by someone waiting for his turn. The scouts make sure that everybody gets a chance to show his stuff.

You may be tempted during these lulls in the action to sit back, and eat some lunch. You may wait for quite some time, but try not to give the impression that baseball isn't uppermost in your mind. Be ready whenever your name is called. Don't be caught chatting on your cellphone, or undressed, or not ready to perform.

A word about hitting

When your turn comes to bat, hit the ball hard and run as fast as you can to first. Don't make hitting complicated. Get a strike you can handle and go to work on it. Don't swing at bad pitches. Even if the pitcher can't find the strike zone, don't feel rushed. *This is your chance to show what you can do.*

There are usually no umpires at tryout camps, so catchers call balls and strikes to keep things moving along. If you swing at bad pitches, though, a scout can only assume that you don't know where the strike zone is.

Watching you bat, the scout is not as interested in whether you get base hits or fly outs as he is in analyzing your swing. He's really looking to see if you have quick hands and good bat speed. Are you keeping your hands back? What about your balance? Do you lunge at off-speed pitches?

Remember that scouts want to see the ball jump off your bat. To that end, there are base hits and there are base hits. The kids who really smack the ball hard are the ones who will be looked at as real prospects. The scouts would rather see two bullet-like groundouts than a flare or soft liner that falls in for a single.

Also, the outcome of your at-bats will not necessarily determine how you are viewed as a prospect. Scouts do not assume that the youngster who hits well in a tryout is a more likely prospect than one who strikes out. After all, the kid who fans twice might be only 17 years old batting against a top college pitcher who's 22. If he has been noticed because he's a terrific middle infielder and runs like the wind, his hitting isn't as important as his defensive tools and foot speed.

By the same token, a youngster might lash two line-drive hits in the tryout. But the scouts may view him as an outfielder who hits line drives rather than home runs and who, unfortunately, doesn't run particularly well. He may be a good hitter, but in terms of an optimal skill combination or the professional "blueprint" scouts rely on, an outfielder who has only average speed and little power isn't likely to fit the ballclub's needs.

For example, most major league clubs want their left and right fielders to be power hitters, able to club 20 or more homers a year. The center fielder is usually speedy—a guy who doesn't normally hit many homers but can steal perhaps 50 bases in a season. Of course, if you have great speed and can hit homers and play a great center field, now you're talking about a budding superstar. But that's rare. Overall, you have to bear in mind what the needs of the organization are in terms of looking at you as a prospect.

In other words, while you observe all the other players go through their paces at the tryout, you will certainly put yourself in the role of scout as well. But as I've tried to point out here, just because a kid hits a couple of ropes in the simulated game doesn't necessarily guarantee him to be a prospect. Likewise, a skinny 17-year-old who has great range, a great glove, and great speed but doesn't hit much might be just the kind of prospect the scout is looking for. In other words, there are a lot of factors that the scout is taking into consideration. All you can control is the impression that you're making.

After The Tryout Is Over

At the end of the day, the head scout will undoubtedly gather the players and thank everyone for coming. He might make general comments about everybody's hard work and the talent he saw on the playing field, but don't expect a specific critique of your individual game. It's not that the scout doesn't care or want to give positive feedback, but it wouldn't be fair to single out only one or two players.

Once the tryout has ended, pack up your things and head on home. Don't wait around to talk to the scout unless he specifically asks you to.

Remember that scouts use tryout camps to bring in talented ballplayers and to see how they've developed over the year and how they compare with other players. As a result, don't expect an immediate call or letter from a scout after a tryout. If he doesn't contact you, wait until the next tryout and repeat your efforts. If you have the tools and attitude that scouts are looking for in professional prospects, you'll make your impression.

Remember this: scouts don't miss much. They're paid to observe everything. And scouts really don't miss too much at tryout camps. What's the best outcome you can expect after a tryout camp? Barring getting signed, if the scout has you fill out that Player Card, that's a good sign. If he asks you about what year you are in school, or for a copy of your team's schedule, these are all good signs as well. In other words, if he comes to you and starts to chat with you, while there's no guarantee that you're going to be signed, you can at least assume that you're now on the scout's radar screen.

A quick review

When the tryout day comes:

- Arrive at the field on time, or even a little early. You're not likely to make a good impression if you are late.
- Bring your own equipment: spikes, gloves, bats, catching gear, even batting helmet. Don't assume anything—bring it all.
- Make certain you're loose. Warm up and then stretch before you start to work out hard. If you've been injured, make sure you tell the scout in charge.
- Wear a sharp, clean uniform. Scouts will form an instant impression based on your appearance.
- Bring a small lunch and something to drink. You are likely to be at the field all day, and it will probably be warm.

- Don't assume there will be a functioning water fountain at the field.
- Hustle. Scouts want to know whether you really want to "play the game." Show them you do by hustling all the time.

Conducting the Tryout

1. Assemble participants on the grass, facing away from the sun. The person in charge should make a few introductory remarks, telling the purpose of the camp. Describe general camp procedure so the players will know what to expect, e.g., warm-up exercises and jogging followed by catch, pepper, infield and outfield, and pitchers' procedures.
2. Have ballplayers line up according to position played, one behind another, with the low number in front as shown on the following chart.

Position

	3B	*SS*	*2B*	*1B*	*C*	*OF*	*P*
Player	3	6	16	11	9	29	20
Number	1	4	12	10	5	27	20

Enter numbers on player evaluation sheets. Make sure that each player knows his number.
3. Ask whether any participant has an injury, sore arm, blisters, or other condition you should know about. Have those players raise their hands, then talk with each individually (don't make them announce their maladies to the whole group).
4. Perform warm-up exercises. Caution the group not to wear themselves out warming up!
  a. Jog around the field.
  b. Do stretching and flexibility exercises.
5. Divide into groups of five or six and play pepper. Pitchers and catchers pair off and warm up.
6. Send pitchers and catchers to bullpen. Scout or designated coach rates pitchers on fastball, curve, etc. Circle the numbers of pitchers who perform best. They will be first to pitch in batting practice. Use radar gun. Be specific.
7. Have remaining players line up in two rows facing each other, 90 feet apart, pair off, and play catch. Tell them to throw overhand and aim

Figure 7–3

chest-high. Scout circulates among players, observing form and arm action, and making appropriate notations on evaluation sheet. Stress playing catch properly (feet, rhythm, constant flex, etc.).

8. Outfielders line up in center field and throw to third base and home. Third baseman and catcher are in position to receive throws. Shortstop positions himself in line with center fielder and third base, arms raised, facing center field. He should not cut off throws, however. Each outfielder makes about five throws, then goes to right field and makes two throws to third, ball hit at the outfielder—then scout should fungo ball down right field line, make outfielder go to the line and throw home.

9. While outfielders are being evaluated, infielders play pepper to warm up.

10. Infielders take their respective positions and scout hits infield. Hit to all positions so the players keep active. Emphasize long throws. Arms are graded best by observing long throws. Use a stopwatch to get times on catchers' throws to second base.

11. After infielders and outfielders have thrown, more all players to 60-yard dash course.

12. Give brief clinic on form running, stressing proper sprinting technique. The course should be laid out along a foul line or other suitable reference line (otherwise, players do not run in a straight line and times are inaccurate). Try to avoid running either with or against the wind; i.e., run at the right angle to the wind.

13. Candidates should run in pairs. Starting position is as in leading off first base (crossover step). Right foot is on the starting line. Pitchers and catchers run first. When they are finished, send in pairs to warm up in the bull pen for batting practice while the rest of the position players run the dash.

Average major league time for 60-yards using the crossover step start is 7.1 seconds.

[NOTE: Have timers start watch on respective runner's initial movement. The timer must force himself to wait until the runner hits the finish line and then stop the watch as fast as he can. By not anticipating the runner, the initial lag is canceled out and the time will be accurate.]

Figure 7–3 (cont.)

14. Call position players in five at a time and begin batting practice. Designate ball shaggers and put two pitchers on the ball bucket, behind second base, to keep the bucket on mound full at all times. Have hitter bunt first two pitches—down the third-base and first-base lines. Next pitch, hit and run; next pitch, move runner from second to third with one out. Then five swings and out—move on to the next hitter.

Each batting practice pitcher should throw to approximately three hitters. The scout, using a radar gun to record pitch speed, should be situated behind the cage to grade pitchers, instruct them on which pitch to throw, etc. This also enables the scout to grade hitters and make sure that proper BP routine is being followed.

Figure 7–3 (cont.)

Running Times and Clocking Players

Our organization believes that SPEED is a vital aspect of a position player's abilities and plays a very important part in the success of a team and a ballclub. Whenever you evaluate a first and a second division club in any league or a successful ballclub with an unsuccessful one, speed plays a prominent role.

Second division clubs are usually handicapped by a lack of speed. Speed plays a very important part not only in the offensive output of a club but also in its defense, particularly in the outfield.

The measurement of actual running speed varies among players and can be very deceptive. For example, a short person usually takes more steps getting to where he wants to go and therefore may give an illusion of a certain level of speed. In actuality, he may only be a fair runner, because he is taking a lot more steps.

On the other hand, the tall guy with long legs and long strides may not look as fast, but may get where he wants to go quicker. To remove any guesswork we put the evaluation of speed on a very technical basis. Therefore, every player must be timed with a stopwatch.

Figure 7–4

Policy
All Players for Draft

60-yard Dash

50	6.9 - 7.0	Average
60	6.8 - 6.7	Above average
70	6.6 - 6.5	Good
80	6.4	Outstanding

Procedure for Clocking Players

Start the clock as soon as the batter makes contact with the ball. You should not wait until contact has been made, but rather let your instinct direct you as to exactly when to start the stopwatch. In other words, it is an instinctive anticipation; as the ball arrives in the hitting zone you will instinctively start the clock. You stop the clock when the batter's foot touches first base.

Listed below is a breakdown of running times and how they fit into the numerical grade of speed. (This scale is used by the Major League Scouting Bureau and a number of other organizations.)

From left side	***From right side***
4.5 - 2	4.6 - 2
4.4 - 3	4.5 - 3
4.3 - 4	4.4 - 4
4.2 - 5	4.3 - 5
4.1 - 6	4.2 - 6
4.0 - 7	4.1 - 7
3.9 - 8	1.0 - 8

Be prepared to clock every runner every time he comes to bat, and record the actual running times on all reports. In addition, list your evaluation of his running speed.

It is possible to see an entire game without getting a true running time on a particular player because he never hits a ball that demands running at full speed. However, you are still to clock all players and record their times. Failure to run out a ball may be an indication of a player's lack of hustle, desire, and makeup. This should be noted.

Figure 7–4 (cont.)

CHAPTER EIGHT

THE TOOLS AND TERMS OF THE TRADE

You will have better insight into what kinds of talents a scout looks for by learning the tools and terms he uses when he scans a ballgame. In this chapter, the major components of the scout's trade are described and their functions explained.

The Scout's Manual: Club Philosophy for Success

The first things a new scout is usually given are the club's scouting manual and an indoctrination into the team's philosophy or blueprint for finding championship major league talent. Before that scout is unleashed to scour a territory for talented young players, he needs to know what he's looking for—or more to the point, what the club's front office is looking for.

There are substantial differences among team blueprints; they are well illustrated by the differences you can observe among the 30 major league clubs. For example, the Yankees traditionally bolster their lineup with longball, and preferably left-handed, power hitters. The Los Angeles Dodgers prefer to build championship teams with power pitchers. And the Cleveland Indians like to have lots of offense in their lineup, in order to take advantage of the friendly confines of Progessive Field.

The top management of each club puts together a composite of what they want, or need, at each position. This "dream team," determined by a variety of factors, is a reflection of the management's philosophy for a pennant-winning ballclub.

Details of this composite are then integrated into the club's scouting manual, so that each scout has a solid idea of the types of prospects to look for. Thus, when I scout a ballplayer, I evaluate him in light of what my organization wants in a prospect. Not every talented player can necessarily meet our needs.

A high school or college player might be considered a terrific prospect by one scout, but not one at all by a scout from a different club. You've probably wondered why some teams follow a certain prospect while others show no interest. Their blueprints are often the reason.

As I scout players it's not enough for me merely to think that a certain young man is a potential professional. I must believe that he has potential not only to make it to the major leagues, but also to win there. That may sound demanding, but as a business, the goal of major league baseball teams is to win the World Series.

As you might suspect, most clubs keep their scouting manuals and blueprints for success top secret. Don't expect a scout to tell you or your coach what those plans are, nor should you ask. Figure 8–1 lists just some of the forms that make up a traditional manual.

By now it should be apparent that a large part of a scout's job is filling out and maintaining forms. But it might surprise you that a scout has to keep up with the paperwork even after a prospect is "signed, sealed, and delivered" to the professional ballclub.

Once a contract is signed, a scout is required to fill out more forms, like the two shown in Figures 8–2 and 8–3. Suppose you had to fill out the "Signed Player's Outline" on yourself. How would you judge a question like best position? If a scout handed you the "Player's Publicity Questionnaire," could you make it impressive and interesting? Personal public relations will become part of the game once you've signed. Questions like your greatest thrill or your most difficult achievement could be grist for media coverage for yourself even now.

A Scout's Notebook: His Bible

Once a scout has a firm sense of what he will be looking for in prospects, he puts together a notebook. That book, which he takes to every game he scouts, contains all the basic and vital information on each player.

In my notebook, I record two sets of information on each player. First, the basic data: height, weight, bats right or left, throws right or left, date of birth, education, and current position. Second are my scouting observations. Does this youngster fit my club's blueprint? To answer that question I have to take note of each young man's physical and psychological tools.

I look at the ballplayer from every perspective. What kind of natural athletic ability does he have? Is he going to grow much taller? Is he likely to put on weight as he matures? Is his body flexible? Does he have the drive to improve? How does he handle adversity on the field? What kind of rapport does he have with his teammates and coach? How about umpires? What about the other team? These questions, and many more, have to be asked—and answered. By the way, as you might imagine, for many of the younger scouts, they prefer to keep their important scouting notes on a laptop. Being more "old school" I

Scouts' Information Forms

u Form letter for schedule and roster request
u Prospect information cards
u Daily game work cards
u Cross-check work pad
u Incentive bonus plan
u Contract tender letter
u Signed player questionnaire
u Player strength and weakness form
u Scouting credits on signed players
u Professional club reports
u Free agent report form
u Non-pro club report
u Professional individual reports
u Cross-check report form
u Professional preferential list
u Secondary phase final summary sheet
u Regular phase final summary sheet
u Final draft cards
u Tryout camp registration cards
u Tryout camp worksheet (pitchers)
u Tryout camp worksheet (players)
u Tryout camp release-from-responsibility letter
u Tryout camp permission letter allowing youngster to participate
u Prospect information form
u Health history
u Signability questionnaire
u Uniform player contracts
u Consent to re-select
u College scholarship plan
u Information request letter

Figure 8–1

Signed Player's Outline

This form is to be prepared by the scout and mailed to the home office along with player contract, or soon thereafter.

Part A

- Player's name
- Position
- Address (city, state, zip code)
- Home telephone (area code)
- Date of birth
- Bats
- Throws
- Glasses/contacts?
- Nationality

Part B

If switch-hitter, hits better from ____________________

If present position is best chance to succeed in pro ball, then state what position you recommend and why: ____________________

____

How many games have you seen him play to date?

High School
College
American Legion
Others

State any injury, illness or physical ailments that may handicap or affect his full potential. List each item and date of injury: ____________________

____

____

Scout's evaluation of above: ____________________

____

____

Figure 8–2

Player's Publicity Questionnaire

This form to be returned with player's contract.

Name ______________________________

Nickname ______________________________

Position ______________ Nationality ______________

Home address ______________________________

city state zip

Telephone ( ) ______________________________

Place of birth ______________________________

city state

Date of birth ______________________________

month day year

Height ______ Weight ______ Hair color ______ Eye color ______

Bat ______________ Throw ______________

Club with which you signed your first professional baseball contract

____

Club scout who signed you date

Circumstances leading to your first contract offer ______________

____

High school attended ______________________________

city state

____

College attended ______________________________

city state

____

year graduated degrees

Figure 8–3

College sports (achievements) ______________________________

____

Is there anyone to whom you particularly owe your success in baseball? Why?

____

Who is your baseball hero? Why? ______________________________

____

Did you play on the same club or in the same league with players now prominent in the major leagues? (club, league, players) ______________

____

Tell about your greatest thrill in baseball ______________________

____

Championship teams on which you have played

____

team name year

Most difficult thing to do in baseball __________________________

____

Hobbies ______________________________________

____

Winter occupation ______________________________

Personal superstitions ______________________________

____

Marital status (wife's name/date of marriage, names/birthdates of children)

____

____

Original baseball position (if position has changed, why? When? By whom?)

____

____

Figure 8–3 (cont.)

keep my notes in an old-fashioned notebook. But no matter what the book is, either handwritten or computerized, the scout keeps all of his vital information close at hand.

The Famous (or Infamous) Radar Gun

The portable radar gun was introduced to professional baseball on a wide scale in the 1970s. Some say that it has revolutionized the profession of scouting, that it has made an art more a science, especially in evaluating pitchers.

Others feel just as strongly that a radar gun, if used improperly, can do as much damage as good for scouting.

The controversy rages on. Certainly, any baseball fan loves to see the gun register in the high 90s for the top hard-throwers in the game today. For the one-in-a-million kid who can fire that high, hard one, the radar gun can instantly confirm a scout's greatest hope—that he really has discovered the next Francisco (K-Rod) Rodriguez or Nolan Ryan.

I view the radar gun as just another scouting tool. I like it and I use it. But I make certain I don't get carried away with its influence. The gun measures only one thing—velocity. Pure, raw velocity. Nothing more. And there's a lot more to a successful pitching prospect than just velocity.

For example, the gun does not measure the ball's movement, or the sharpness of a curve or a slider, or the pitch's location on the plate. All it does is measure velocity, and velocity alone cannot guarantee a contract. For every Justin Verlander or Josh Beckett in the majors, there are dozens of unknown pitchers in the low minors who can throw just as hard but who never conquer the finer points of pitching.

Pitching coaches on the major league level will tell you that to be a winner, a pitcher must have movement on the ball. It's always more difficult for a batter to make contact with a pitch that comes in at, say, 88 mph but sinks down or shoots away than to hit a 94-mph fastball that is as straight as an arrow.

Why? Simple physics. A batter has greater eye-to-hand motor control with a pitch that comes in a straight line, no matter how fast it comes. He might swing a little late or foul the ball back, but an experienced hitter will adjust for the increased speed, choke up a little on the bat, and then hit the next straight fastball right on the money.

In contrast, the ball that comes in slower but has great—and unpredictable—movement is more difficult to hit, because the movement adds a new variable to the eye-to-hand control required. Not only must the batter cope with the velocity of the pitch, he must also track the ball's movement to make contact.

And there's no predictability to the pitches—one may sink down while the next one moves away.

It's easier to hit a ball that's always going to be in the same place, regardless of the pitch's velocity, than it is to hit a pitch that's always moving. This is obvious to most followers of baseball, but it bears repeating when it comes to radar guns.

It's well accepted in scouting circles that different guns are calibrated in different ways. As a result, one radar gun may clock a pitch at 90 mph while a different gun measures the same pitch at 86 or 87 mph.

A few miles per hour may not seem like a big difference, but in scouting a pitching prospect, 3–4 mph might determine whether or not a contract is offered. So you can see that the accuracy of a radar gun is crucial.

I feel that the use of the radar gun has been great for baseball and for scouting. It adds precision, and I have found it particularly helpful in clocking pitchers at night or in a gym; when watching a pitcher under artificial light, the user's perception of a pitch's velocity can be thrown off. The radar gun gives a scout a relative standard of how hard a young man is throwing.

Sometimes a radar gun will flash two speeds. One speed appears on the screen then quickly disappears to be replaced by a second reading. In a case like this the radar gun has recorded two speeds. The first number is the speed of the ball as it leaves the pitcher's hand. The second number, which most scouts refer to, is the maximum velocity the ball reaches on its flight to the plate. That maximum speed might occur when the ball is halfway to the plate, three-quarters of the way there, or even as it crosses the plate. Most physics experts agree that the pitch reaches a top speed and then actually slows down a bit by the time it reaches the batter.

I have mentioned that I look upon the radar guns as just another part of my scouting repertoire. In recent years, I have used the gun to measure not only pitching velocity, but the relative strength of outfielders and infielders. How better to find out just how strong a fielder's arm is than by clocking a throw with a radar gun? Here again, though, the gun can measure velocity, and nothing more. A shortstop might have a tremendously strong arm, but if he can't throw accurately across the diamond, he won't be considered a prospect. The scout still must determine the many factors beyond velocity.

The Scout's Stopwatch

Every scout carries a stopwatch. Like a radar gun, a stopwatch measures raw speed, and for that it is invaluable. But just as a radar gun cannot measure a pitch's movement or location, a stopwatch cannot measure what kind of jump a basestealer gets on a pitcher or what kinds of instincts a runner has on the base paths.

Nonetheless, determining a player's running speed is essential. Raw speed is one of those tools that really cannot be taught, although you may be able to improve your speed through diligent exercise (see Chapter Five). Scouts love to see a young man with speed to burn. Players like Jose Reyes, B.J. Upton, and Ichiro Suzuki have shown that leg speed can really break a game open offensively. And although players can somewhat improve their foot speed, those who are blessed with superior speed are hard to find. That's why they are so valuable to any team.

Timing baserunning and fielding

Scouts time each batter when he comes to the plate. Clocking a player's run from home to first base gives the scout a fairly good idea of how fast he is. Scouts have developed a standard scale for a home-to-first run: the major league average for a right-handed batter (clocked from the time the bat makes contact with the ball) is 4.3 seconds. For left-handed hitters, the average is 4.2 seconds.

Those numbers can give you a goal to work toward. Get a stopwatch and have a coach, a parent, or a friend time you. Remember to pay close attention when starting the clock—begin when you hit the ball, not when you swing the bat.

Speed plays a major role in baseball. Most casual fans think of speed only in connection with stealing a base. But speed has many different applications. How many times have you seen a quick-legged center fielder like Carlos Beltran or Aaron Rowand race down a well-hit fly ball and turn a "sure" double into a long out? That's speed at work.

The speed of a lead-off hitter like Juan Pierre influences the play of a game. Because he runs so well, the infielders have to play a little closer to the plate than usual. The defensive players also know that on a close play, such as a ground ball in the hole or a bunt, they will have to rush their throws a bit because of Juan's speed. Rushing a play, of course, dramatically increases the chances for a mistake or fielding error. Again, the ability to run makes the difference.

There are many other illustrations of the importance of speed in baseball. A fleet-footed outfielder can keep a ball in the gap to a long single if he is fast enough to cut the ball off. A fast baserunner can take the extra base—instead of stopping at second he can chance going on to third. A hitter who runs well can prevent a double play by getting down the line to first.

If you are being scouted in a game, make certain you run out every fly ball, grounder, hit—everything—as hard and as fast as you can.

Why? Because a scout can only judge what you do, not what you say: that point cannot be overemphasized. You may be quick on your feet, but unless you show me you can really move, I won't mark it down on my notebook. If speed is one of your assets, be aggressive: show me you can run. Once is all it will take to get my attention.

Some scouts like to time runners from first to third. Others prefer to get a reading on how long it takes you to run a complete lap around all the bases at top speed. A scout might also use that exercise to see if you know how to cut a base or how to hit the bag with your foot and then push off for greater acceleration.

Putting catchers on the clock

Stopwatches are also used to clock a catcher's throw to second base. Major league scouts know that unless a catcher can catch a pitch and make the throw to second in 1.8 or 2.0 seconds, he will have difficulty throwing out professional basestealers.

Here's the breakdown: The stopwatch starts at the instant the catcher receives the pitch. It is stopped just as the ball reaches second. The throw has to be accurate, right on the money.

This timing is essential, because some catchers have terrifically strong arms but take too much time getting the ball out of their gloves and making their throws. At the other end of the spectrum might be a player whose arm is only so-so, but who gets rid of the ball in a hurry. The clock tells the scout just how a particular catcher might fare against a talented runner.

Scouts realize that most baserunners steal on the pitcher, not the catcher. To compensate for that, a scout will time the entire battery; that is, he'll start his stopwatch when the pitcher comes out of his stretch and makes the pitch to home. The clock stops once the ball reaches second base, after the catcher has fired the ball down there. The total time a scout accepts for all this is 3.3—3.5 seconds. Why? Because the typical basestealer in the major leagues takes that long to get from first to second on an attempted steal.

There are other variables involved in basestealing. Some pitchers throw harder than others. A fastball coming in at 90 mph gets to the catcher a lot faster than a slow curve at 75 mph. That's one reason it's better to try to steal on a curveball pitcher than on a hard thrower.

Although the typical basestealer needs approximately 3.5 seconds to go from first to second, some guys, like Ichiro Suzuki, are consistently clocked at 3.3 seconds or less. That may not seem like a substantial difference. But it's only

90 feet—thirty yards—between first and second, and .2 seconds can make a dramatic difference when you need that stolen base.

The Follow-Up File

Each scout has a system for keeping files on prospects; next to my scouting notebook, those files are my most treasured possession.

I have described how I gather lineups and make individualized notes on each player who participates in a game I observe as a scout. That evening I go over the day's notes. I review the observations I've made, and make any other notations that come to mind. Figure 8–4 shows some typical comments.

Follow-Up Report

Why this player should be followed:

Player 1.
Average build, average body. Smooth, efficient, quick catching actions; quick release with average arm and accuracy when needed; heady receiver, handler of pitches.

Lacks strength at present to hit longball; rakes at ball; body and size indicate limited stamina and durability.

Watch closely for development, especially strength through maturity.

Player 2.
Tall, raw-boned, good pitcher's body; average major league velocity with loose arm. Does not use mound well for leverage, dead front side. No pull, rushes; potential tremendous mechanical adjustment. Little deception in delivery; fastball straight. Hits lot of bats, but with playing time, pro improvement and instruction can take off.

Watch closely for improvement. Possible transfer to other school.

Player 3.
No known injuries, medium build, compact, strong; loose, live, rubber-armed reliever; low 3/4; fastball sinks, tails well; curveball deceptive; hides ball.

Fastball lacks major league velocity. Curveball not tight. Only merits watching to see if fastball improves.

Figure 8–4

For example, I might have seen a talented center fielder whose speed impressed me. But he's only a sophomore in high school, and not eligible to be signed. I write his name, position, high school, and so on, on a follow-up card and file it away. Since this youngster has two more years of high school, I would file him in my card deck for the next spring.

Or I might have seen a third baseman with quickness and range but only an average arm. He's a senior with some hitting tools and, judging from my notes, might be a sleeper of a prospect—not as a third baseman but rather at second. Again, I file all his vital information on a follow-up card.

However, since this player is a senior and eligible for the free agent draft, I place his card in my special follow-up file for this year. I review that file weekly because I must go back and watch the youngsters in it soon, before the draft. Then if I still think a certain player is a prospect, I will contact a cross-checker to come see him play.

As you can imagine, my filing system becomes quite crowded by the end of the school year, after I have seen hundreds of high school, junior college, and college games. Not only do I keep each game on record, but I also write up a card on every ballplayer who catches my eye.

Although this is my own system for keeping track of hundreds of prospects I see, each scout undoubtedly develops his own.

You can see why it's so important that you show your skills when a scout is watching. A tip-off to your abilities through a newspaper story or from a coach or even an umpire probably brought him to your game. But from that point on, you have to show your stuff.

If you have outstanding speed, show it. If you have a great arm from the outfield, make certain you show it during practice and, if the chance arises, during the game. If you have a masterful curveball, make sure you throw it—and throw it for strikes. My point is simple: Just show me once that you can hit a ball 450 feet, or that you can run to first in less than four seconds, or that you can throw a pitch 90 mph, and believe me, your name will be on the follow-up list.

And once you're on that list, you're guaranteed that I'll be back to see you again. And that's the first step on the road to getting signed.

CHAPTER NINE

EXTRA INNINGS: COMMON QUESTIONS ANSWERED

In my years of playing, coaching, and scouting the sport of professional baseball, I've heard just about every question you could possibly imagine from baseball prospects. In the previous chapters, the answers to many of these various questions can be found. However, to tie up any loose ends or lingering uncertainties, I want to address some of the most common questions I hear from ballplayers.

Question: *Are there particular programs in which a high school senior or junior college player can make himself known to college coaches and pro scouts?*
For years, most college coaches and, to a lesser degree, pro scouts have relied upon networks of contacts. Coaches, having to recruit new players each year, often call upon fellow colleagues, high school and American Legion coaches, local sportswriters, alumni, and anyone else they think may be able to recommend an outstanding high school player.

Once a player has been identified as a potential prospect, the coach ordinarily dispatches an assistant coach to watch the youngster play. If the assistant feels that the youngster is good enough to warrant consideration, then the head coach will generally come to watch him play and perhaps offer him a scholarship at that point.

As you can imagine, such a system of contacts and follow-up can be haphazard. In fact, most college coaches would tell you that recruiting talented players depends mostly on luck—being in the right place at the right time. It is ironic that although championship college ballclubs are built upon talented players, there isn't a very systematic way of letting those coaches know about good high school players.

Question: *What if I just get myself into shape and go to some spring training sites in Florida and Arizona—will the pros give me a tryout down there?*
In most cases, if you just show up at a spring training site and ask for a tryout, you'll be turned away. At best, you'll be told about the next open tryout camp

in or near your hometown.

Occasionally, a few clubs, like the St. Louis Cardinals and the Kansas City Royals, stage open tryouts for one morning during spring training. On that morning anyone can come and try out in front of the scouts. To learn the dates and locations of these tryouts write to these clubs during the winter months and ask.

Question: *How about if I go directly to a Class A or AA club and ask the manager for a tryout?*
You'll probably run into the same kind of closed door as you would in spring training. Unless you're a former minor leaguer who already has a release, the manager will probably tell you that he's sorry, but due to the insurance risks or major league club policy, he can't allow you to try out.

I'm certain that on rare occasions someone has asked for a tryout and been given one and even has signed, but the odds of that happening are extremely low. For better or worse, minor league clubs tend to insulate themselves from "walk-ons."

If you have played pro ball before, the manager will most likely call his front office and ask for a computer printout on you and your abilities from the club's scouting system. If the report is negative or lukewarm, you'll probably be told thanks, but no thanks. However, if the report is a good one, you might be allowed to try out.

Question: *If I contact the major league clubs personally, will they send a scout to see me play?*
First of all, if you do contact a major league club, make certain you write rather than call. Most scouts work out of their homes, so a phone call to the club's front office will likely be a dead-end. But ballclubs are good at corresponding by mail, so your chances of getting a response are better if you write.

Be sure to enclose a self addressed, stamped envelope with your inquiry. In your letter, ask when and where they plan to hold a tryout camp in your area. If you decide to send some clippings of your best games, a half dozen or fewer should get your point across.

At this juncture, information is all you can reasonably request of a ballclub. But by taking the time to write, you should hear in a few weeks about as many as 12 to 16 tryout camps, all of which you'll be invited to attend.

Question: *Where do I get names and addresses for the clubs?*

For a complete listing of all thirty major league clubs, their addresses and website information, refer to the Appendix.

Question: *What is the difference between a "co-op" team and an "independent" club in the minors?*

A co-op, or cooperative team, is a professional ballclub that has on its roster ballplayers whose contracts are owned by major league ballclubs. Say the Appalachian League has a co-op team playing in Bristol, Virginia. On that ballclub, you might find six players whose contracts belong to the Detroit Tigers, seven players owned by the St. Louis Cardinals, and nine who are part of the New York Mets organization.

The reason they are all thrown together in one club is that their own ballclubs don't have enough roster spaces on their other minor league affiliates for them to play there. Rather than having such players idle or releasing them, the various front offices have placed them on a co-op team.

Most major league clubs would prefer to have all their kids play on the club's own minor league teams. But if a system is overstocked with players, a co-op is a very logical and convenient solution, allowing these 20 or so players a chance to play pro ball on a daily basis.

In contrast to a co-op, an independent club is made up of ballplayers who do not have contracts with any major league team. Instead, their contracts are with the individual owner of the independent club, and each ballplayer is employed by and paid by that owner.

These days, there are more independent teams and independent leagues than there have been in more than 30 years. That means there are even more jobs open than ever if you want to play pro ball. For a complete listing, get a copy of *Baseball America*'s annual almanac to find out about the different leagues and opportunities.

If you feel that you've been overlooked by the major league scouts, and you still want to play professional ball, signing with an independent club will give you all the experiences of playing minor league ball. But keep in mind that an independent club is nothing more than a showcase for your diamond talents—a good year there doesn't guarantee that you'll be signed by a major league club.

If you belong to, say, the Pittsburgh Pirates and have an excellent year in Class A ball, there's every expectation that you'll be moved to Class AA the next spring. But with an independent club, there's really no progression or ladder to climb. It's just one club in one league with one owner.

On the bright side, you will be playing ball in a professional setting, and occasionally a player from an independent club will be seen, scouted, and signed by one of the major league clubs. But, once again, this is more the exception than the rule, and the scouts know it.

But you never know what might happen once you're in a professional arena. A few years ago, when I was coaching in the Atlantic Collegiate Baseball League, our team had a bright, affable left-hander named Rob Nelson who was a top-notch pitcher at Cornell. Like everybody else, he was looking to get signed.

Unfortunately, Nelson never got drafted. But he decided he wanted to go play pro ball and hooked up with an independent team in Portland, Oregon. Rob had a relatively undistinguished career in pro ball, but one evening while sitting in the bullpen with former major leaguer Jim Bouton, who was also on the club, the two developed the concept for a new product called "Big League Chew."

Big League Chew, which as you probably know is bubble gum shreds that resemble chewing tobacco and comes in a foil packet, got its start in that bullpen in Portland. While Rob Nelson never got to the majors as a pitcher, the annual income from his and Bouton's Big League Chew affords him a major league salary.

Question: *Some kids play ball overseas, such as in Italy or Holland. Is that another way of being seen by the scouts?*

No, not really. If you opt to play ball in Italy, Holland, Australia, South Africa, or even Mexico or Japan, you're actually limiting your chances of being scouted. While playing ball in another country can be a great deal of fun, if you are trying to make a forward step into a professional career, you're more or less going in the wrong direction. As you can probably see, most of the top foreign players are trying to come here to play pro ball—not stay where they are.

True, there are some exceptions to this. Some players who can't get signed after playing college baseball in the U.S. end up playing in a foreign country and then come back to play pro ball here, but this is very rare indeed.

If you really want to pursue a pro career in baseball, stay in the U.S. and play for an indy team if no affiliated team will sign you. Most guys who play in Italy, Holland, Korea, and so on are fellows who have already played pro ball here in the U.S.

Question: *Why do the scouts at tryout camps rarely give anybody a pat on the back?*

It's not that scouts are naturally mean tempered, or that they always get up on the wrong side of the bed, or that they don't recognize when a youngster makes an outstanding play or hits a pitch right on the button. It's just that a tryout camp is more or less an audition session, and scouts tend to say little to the ballplayers in attendance because that's appropriate to the situation.

Why is that? Imagine how you would feel if a scout came over to the player next to you and started praising him to the sky, telling him that he was a real prospect, a real potential major leaguer. Naturally, you would expect the scout to say the same kinds of things to you. But suppose he didn't. He complimented your colleague and then looked at you and said nothing, or said things that weren't as complimentary. You'd come away thinking that the scout either didn't know what he was doing or that he was a real jerk. Either way, you would be hurt, unmotivated, and angry at the scout and his organization. Thus, to avoid hurt feelings and damage to public relations, scouts at tryout camps rarely say anything complimentary.

If the scout is thinking to himself that you're a real find, he'll put your name in his book to follow up. Even though you're accustomed to hearing instant positive feedback from your coach or teammates for a play well made, don't assume the worst if a scout says nothing; in a tryout camp, that doesn't necessarily mean you're not a prospect.

Question: *What if my dad or mom talks to the scout after my tryout?*
My colleagues tend to be split on the issue of inquiring parents. Some scouts feel that parents have no right to interfere with a scout's analysis of their ballplaying son. Others feel that parents shouldn't get involved until the scout's organization has decided to make an offer to a youngster.

The attitude of these scouts is this: Do your parents go and sit on a job interview with you? Do they ask the interviewer if you got the job? While this attitude may seem harsh, you can understand that it is time-consuming for scouts to answer all the questions that interested parents have about their son's ability.

However, being a parent myself, I can certainly understand the concerns and interest that a father or mother may show for their young ballplayer. When a parent approaches me after a tryout camp or at a game to ask my professional opinion about his or her son's potential as a prospect, I will typically give it.

I'm not suggesting that you should urge mom and dad to stroll over to the scouts and start asking about your ability. The last thing you want is a notation in the scout's notebook that your parents are "pushy" or "nosy."

But if a parent comes up to me and wants an answer to a specific question or two, I'll be as cordial as my time allows. For example, parents may ask whether I believe their son is good enough to play baseball in a major college program, or whether he'd be better off going to a Division III school or junior college instead. Or they might ask whether I think their son truly has a chance in the free agent draft or if he should think about attending college in the fall.

These kinds of questions are legitimate ones, and as a scout and father, I feel they deserve honest answers. After all, if I don't tell parents the truth as I see it, they may allow their son to pursue a goal that is either unreachable or, at best, blocked by major obstacles. The answers may not be the ones the parents or son want to hear. A father may want to hear that his son is going to be a top draft choice and future major leaguer. But if I feel that his son won't be drafted any higher than the 20th round, for example, I feel obligated to tell him so.

Naturally, I'll cushion my answer so as not to embarrass myself or the father. For example, I may say that there are 29 other teams who might feel differently about his son's draftability than I do. But there's really no reason or motivation for me to give a parent anything but my honest assessment. Particularly when the picture is clouded by potential college scholarship offers and the like, the decision is too important to be sidestepped by a scout.

If your parents really want to address a scout about your ability, they should be prepared to ask specific questions. Inquiries such as, "What do you think of my son?" or "Did you know my boy was selected all-league this year?" are likely to bring a menacing glance from any scout. But if your mom or dad approaches the scout in a more direct, common sense manner, chances are they'll get a decent response.

Question: *How about if I go up to a major league scout myself and ask for an evaluation of my abilities?*
Chances are that you'll get the same kind of reaction as was just described. That is, if you are courteous, polite, professional, and specific in your questioning, the scout will probably give you specific answers.

By the same token, if you merely ask the scout for his overall opinion of your athletic abilities, he's liable to be somewhat vague and noncommittal. And he may even tell you things that you didn't ask to hear, such as he's not interested in signing you.

However, as I pointed out earlier, particularly if you're a senior in college, you have little to lose by approaching a scout. If you decide on this kind of direct approach, tell the scout exactly what your status is and how much you really want to play pro ball.

Some years ago a very talented lefty first baseman named Mark Bingham played at Harvard University. Bingham, who stands 6-foot-6, had been drafted out of high school by the Cincinnati Reds and supposedly turned down a bonus of nearly $40,000 to attend Harvard. Although Mark had an outstanding career there, for some reason the New England scouts never drafted him, and by the time he graduated, he was ready to give up his hopes of playing professional ball. But as one last shot, Bingham contacted me and asked me directly if I might be interested in signing him.

I had known about Mark since his high school days and had followed his success into his college years. As it turned out, the Angels needed a left-handed first sacker for one of their rookie clubs. I made a call to the club's front office, got their approval, and within 24 hours of his call, Mark was offered a pro contract. That summer he was named to the All-Star squad in the Northwest League.

Mark Bingham's story isn't unique. Ray Chadwick, a right-handed pitcher for the Angels, pitched in the majors for the first time in the summer of 1985. Ray had been an outstanding football defensive back at Winston-Salem State in North Carolina. Unfortunately, the school didn't have a baseball program, so he was unable to play that sport in college.

However, a few years later—while Ray was working as a member of the grounds crew for the Winston-Salem Red Sox in the Class A Carolina League—the word got around that he had been a pretty respectable pitcher back in high school.

Angels' scout Alex Cosmidis was one of those who heard this tip, and Ray and Alex talked baseball. After a few workouts, Alex made a recommendation that the Angels draft and sign Ray, which they did. An unusual story, but a true one.

Question: *What if I'm invited to an MLSB tryout?*
By all means, go, and take the tryout seriously. Remember that your goal is to get on some ballclub's follow-up list. If you do well for the MLSB, your abilities will be reported to the Bureau's headquarters and there is a good chance that the 30 major league club scouting directors will see your name and numbers.

If a scout from the MLSB asks you to fill out a card make sure to do so. The card will ask for the same basic information that was listed on a typical card from a regular scout (Chapter Two, Figure 2–2). That card will go back to the MLSB front office, be put into a computer, and then be sent out to the major league teams. From there, each team can send its own scout to follow up. You can never tell what's going to happen at a MLSB tryout. A few years ago, a young hard-throwing right-hander named Rob Semerano was invited to attend a tryout by Pat Shortt, a long-time MLSB scout. Semerano was playing for the Stamford Robins in the Atlantic Collegiate Baseball League, where he was throwing bullets. Curiously, though, Semerano didn't pitch much at Fordham

University, so he was something of an unknown quantity. But on that hot summer day at the tryout, in front of a dozen scouts, Semerano consistently hit 95 mph on the radar gun. That got him on the scouts' map, and he ultimately was drafted and signed by the Oakland Athletics.

Question: *What if I have a "bad day" at an MLSB tryout camp—does that mean that a negative report will be sent to all thirty teams?*
MLSB scouts are not so much interested in whether you get a base hit or strike out two batters in a row at a tryout camp. Rather, MLSB scouts, like all scouts, are looking for evidence of a player's physical tools—the tools a prospect needs to make it to the majors. Hence, your individual performance, while certainly noticed, is not as important as your skills: running, throwing, bat speed, pitching control, and velocity. Remember, these are the tools MLSB scouts are looking for.

Can an MLSB scout actually sign a player? No, because he's not working for just one club. But on the other hand, some scouts from the Bureau carry tremendous weight and enjoy great respect from the various ballclubs, and some clubs will gamble on a prospect just because they value that MLSB scout's opinion.

Question: *Sometimes a scout tells a ballplayer that he's definitely going to be drafted, but he isn't. How and why does that happen?*
Unless you're considered by all the scouts and all the major scouting publications to be a definite first-round pick, don't assume that you're going to get drafted. The stands are full of guys who were told directly by one scout or another that they would definitely be drafted. Then draft day comes, and the telephone never rings.

So while it's nice to hear a scout tell you or your parents that you're a lock to be drafted, it's never a sure thing until you get that actual phone call from the team's front office, confirming your selection.

Why would a scout be tempted to tell you all this in the first place? That's difficult to say. Perhaps he has so befriended you and your family that in his enthusiasm he has proclaimed, "You're definitely going to be drafted!" even when he should know better than to make such promises.

Or, maybe the scout tells you that you're going to be drafted just so he can then ask, "Tell me, how much would it take to sign you?" By making you feel good and then asking your price, he's straying into what most scouts would consider unethical territory. But "signability" is a big issue for scouts. They need to be able to go back to their bosses and tell them honestly what kind of bonus money the kid (and his family) is looking for. Bear in mind that only the kids in rounds 1 through 10 ever get much of a bonus—and usually it's only the first- or second-rounders who get the millions for just signing their name. But for lots of kids and their parents, if he's drafted out of high school, the first thing he wants is enough money to cover four years of college. That can run into the low six-figures in a hurry, and in truth, very few clubs can, or will, offer that kind of money to an 18-year-old. It's a tough, tough choice to make for any youngster who wants to pursue his dream.

In any event, sometimes the scout honestly feels that you're going to be drafted and says so. He bases his opinion on the fact that you're the top-rated player on his prospect list. But even that can be misleading, and the scout should know better. As you have read earlier, each scout has a list of top players. But maybe the cross-checker has watched you play and considers you no better than 20th or 25th overall on his master list, even though you're the best prospect in your area.

As a result, by the time the other top prospects have been drafted, your name may fall to the bottom and maybe even off the list, and you don't get drafted. As such, if you told your friends that you're going to be drafted and then you're not, well, you're going to be embarrassed. Better to say nothing until it happens. Again, don't presume anything until the draft comes and you're actually asked to sign.

Question: *Is it a good idea not to give your real age?*

You may have heard old stories about players who shaved years off their age to convince managers that they were younger than was true. Lots of players over the years are famous for not giving their correct ages. Even Danny Almonte, the infamous over-age Little League pitcher, was caught when it turned out that he was really older than what his birth certificate said.

A ballplayer's age is vitally important to a scout, because all of his calculations and projections about your development are based on what you can do now and your current age. In other words, if you show talents and abilities at age 18 that are more common to a 21-year-old, the scout bases his predictions on that.

By the same token, if you're already 23 and the scout compares your abilities to those of a typical 19-year-old, that affects his evaluation differently. Hence, a player's age is crucial to a scout's judgment, which is why many ballplayers are tempted to subtract a year or two from their real ages.

But you can understand that a scout would be distressed by a youngster who tried to lie about his birth date or age. As far as scouts are concerned, any time you mislead them or present confusing information about your personal life, you become more of a suspect than a prospect. For example, just recently there was a major scandal about a young prospect from the Dominican Republic in the Nationals' organization who signed for a $1.4 million bonus. It was only discovered after he had signed that he had used a forged birth certificate and a fake name, and that he was really four years older than he had told the scouts. This player's status in pro ball is now in serious jeopardy, and the Nationals are still looking at their options regarding the bonus money. Unfortunately, this practice of using fake birth certificates and lying about one's age has taken place a lot with players from the Dominican Republic, where record-keeping is not very accurate. But it has happened with other prospects from other countries as well.

Quite simply, don't lie or make any misleading statements to scouts. Besides, these days, thanks to computerized record checking not only here in the U.S., but around the world, it's exceedingly difficult for a young player to shave a year or two off his age and get away with it.

Question: *Why do so many players get drafted, play for a year, and then get released?*
One of the realities of the business side of professional baseball is the limitation of open spots on a roster. The typical major league ballclub has AAA or AA clubs, one or two Class A clubs, and probably a short-season rookie team.

Look at the numbers: In the minors, most clubs are limited to 22 to 25 active players. That means that from top to bottom, the entire roster of players in one major league system might break down like this:

Major league roster: 25
AAA roster: 23
AA roster: 22–23
Class A Rosters (2 teams): 50
Rookie team roster: 30–40
Total: 149–160

The numbers start to get crunched each spring when a new draft is announced. Let's say a typical ballclub drafts 50 new players, of which 30 sign contracts to play. Then perhaps 10 more new players are signed as free agents.

Now the club has a total of 40 new faces, and they want to see them play. A little arithmetic tells you that if 40 new kids are signed, 40 "old" kids have to be released. Because the more talented and proven players are in AAA and AA ball, most clubs release kids from Class A and rookie ball. I would say that about 90 percent of all pro players never get out of Class A or Rookie Ball. Yep, it's that tough.

The turnover rate is about 20 percent each spring—quite high for most businesses. But in baseball, it's the only way to stay in the business.

Question: *Should a player sign right out of high school or play college ball?*
This is a difficult question to answer, because each ballplayer is different from the next. Some kids are definitely better off signing now, while some others are better off waiting. However, the longer a ballplayer waits to play against professional competition, the longer it will take to get to the big leagues.

Here are some of the factors you and your family should take into consideration in making your decision:

How high a draft choice are you? If you're a top draft choice and the club is offering you a substantial signing bonus, then the issue is primarily economic.

Has your physical development peaked? Most ballplayers, at 18 or 19, still have more growing to do. If you don't feel that you've fully matured when offered a contract, perhaps you ought to think about playing college ball for the next few years. Remember, you can always sign after you finish college.

Are you college material academically? If not, you might want to sign now and get a start in pro ball. In other words, if you're not a very good student, attending college just to play ball will not be much motivation in the classroom. As such, before you opt to sign a contract, if you have the option of attending college or junior college, be sure to weigh all of your options.

Question: *What kinds of questions should a high school or junior college player ask of a college coach who comes to recruit?*
Assuming that you're satisfied with the school's academic opportunities and campus life—and those are vitally important considerations—the first question I would ask is, "What are my chances of becoming a starter on your club *this year*?"

You should go on to ask him how many other players he's recruiting at your position, who played your position last season, and how many guys at your position are ahead of you; that is, if you're a freshman second baseman, is the incumbent second baseman a senior or a sophomore?

If the player at your position is only one year ahead, you don't want to sit on the pines waiting for a chance to play only in your senior year. You should also ask how much of an athletic scholarship you will be receiving, and also whether you will be on the team's travel squad. These may seem like obvious questions, but too many incoming players are too embarrassed to ask them. If you find that you have difficulty in asking the coach these questions in person, simply have your parent or your high school coach email the questions to the college coach so that you have the college coach's answer in writing.

Also, ask about the practice schedule, the team's fall and spring game schedules, the off-season weight or conditioning regimen, and any spring trip to the South. Ask any questions you have, and make certain you get answers you can understand. Selecting a college may be one of the most important decisions you make in life, so take your time and get all the information you need.

Question: *Is minor league ball as rough as people say it is?*
Another difficult question. In general, it's true that playing minor league ball is not very comfortable.

The stories about all-night bus rides, eating in cheap restaurants, and staying in cheap motels are for the most part true. And the pay in the low minors isn't great.

But despite the obstacles, I've found that every young man who ever signed and played pro ball wouldn't have passed up that experience for anything in the world. Remember, you're getting paid to play baseball—and for most ballplayers, that's a dream come true. (By the way, for an excellent account of what minor league life is like, pick up a copy of *Harvard Boys* by John and Rick Wolff.)

Question: *What is the role of the scout after he signs a ballplayer?*
A scout likes to keep track of his signees. He may talk to a ballplayer weekly by telephone or keep track of his statistics through the club's front office. Scouts take great pride in the players they sign, and certainly enjoy it whenever a young pro takes the time to keep up the communication.

APPENDIX A

MAJOR LEAGUE DRAFT RULES

Eligibility

In order to be drafted a player must fit the following criteria:

a) Be a resident of the United States, Canada, or a U.S. territory such as Puerto Rico. Players from other countries are not subject to the draft, and can be signed by any team.
b) Never before been signed a major or minor league contract.
c) High school players are eligible only after graduation, and if they have not attended college.
d) Players at four-year colleges are eligible after completing their junior years, or after their 21st birthdays. The exception to this is Division III schools, where players can be drafted before their junior year.
e) Junior and community college players are eligible to be drafted at any time.

Draft Order

The general draft order is the reverse order of the previous year's standings. If two teams finish with identical records, the previous year's standings of the two teams is the tiebreaker, with the team having a worse record receiving the higher pick.

Negotiating Rights

Prior to 2007, a team retained the rights to sign a selected player until one week prior to the next draft, or until the player enters, or returns to, a four-year college on a full-time basis. Starting in 2007, the deadline for signing a drafted player became August 15. A selected player who enters a junior college cannot be signed until the conclusion of the school's baseball season. A player who is drafted and does not sign with the club that selected him may be drafted again at a future year's draft, so long as the player is eligible for that year's draft. A club may not select a player again in a subsequent year, unless the player has consented to the re-selection.

A player who is eligible to be selected and is passed over by every club becomes a free agent. He may sign with any club, up until one week before the next draft, or until the player enters, or returns to, a four-year college full-time or enters, or returns to, a junior college. In the one-week period before any draft, which is called the "closed period," the general rule is that no club may sign a new player.

Compensatory Picks

Teams can earn Compensatory picks in the draft based on departing free agents. Free agents are ranked by the Elias Sports Bureau based on their previous two years of playing, and against players of similar positions. Players are categorized as Class A, Class B, or they fall into the category of all other players. Below is a description of each free agent class and the compensation the free agent's former team received when the player signs with a different team.

Class A free agents are ranked in the top 20 percent of players at their positions. A team that signs a Type A player gives its top draft pick to the club that the player is leaving. The "losing" club also receives a supplemental pick in the "sandwich" round between the first and second rounds.

Class B free agents are ranked below the top 20 percent but in the top 40 percent of players at their positions. A team that loses a Type B player receives a supplemental pick, but the signing team does not lose any picks.

All other players carry no compensation at all. There had previously been a third class of "Type C" players, but that was eliminated in the new CBA.

To earn a compensatory pick, a free agent must either be signed before the arbitration deadline in early December, or be offered arbitration by their former team but still sign with someone else.

Compensatory picks that one team gives another via this method are the highest available pick that team has. If a team owes two other teams draft picks via Type A free agents, the team whose departing player had a higher score gets the higher ranked pick. A team cannot lose picks it has earned via compensation. Also, the first 15 picks in the draft cannot be lost via compensation, so a team that is in that rank would give up their second-round pick.

The order of the supplemental round between the first and second rounds is determined by inverse order of the previous year's standings. All the Type A picks are done first, and then the order resets for all the Type B compensation picks.

Teams can also earn compensation for unsigned picks from the previous year's draft. If a team doesn't sign a first- or second-round pick, they will get to pick at the same slot plus one the following year. For instance, if the team with the fifth overall pick does not sign that player, they would have the sixth overall pick the following year. The regular draft order would continue around those picks. As compensation for not signing a third-round pick, teams would get a pick in a supplemental round between the third and fourth rounds. If a team fails to sign a player with one of these compensated picks, there is no compensation the following year.

For more detailed information about the draft be sure to visit:
www.MiLB.com
www.BaseballAmerica.com
www.BaseballBlueBook.com

APPENDIX B

MAJOR LEAGUE TEAM ADDRESSES AND WEBSITES

For the most up-to-date contact info for all major league teams visit: http://mlb.mlb.com/team

Major League Baseball
350 Park Avenue
New York, NY 10022
mlb.com

Major League Scouting Bureau
3500 Porsche Way
Suite 100
Ontario, CA 91764
(909) 980–1881

National League

Arizona Diamondbacks
Chase Field
401 East Jefferson Street
Phoenix, AZ 85001
Phone: (602) 462–6500
dbacks.com
losdbacks.com

Atlanta Braves
Turner Field
755 Hank Aaron Drive
Atlanta, GA 30315
Phone: (404) 522–7630
braves.com
bravesbeisbol.com

Chicago Cubs
Wrigley Field
1060 West Addison
Chicago, IL 60613–4397
Phone: (773) 404–2827
cubs.com
loscubs.com

Cincinnati Reds
Great American Ball Park
100 Main Street
Cincinnati, OH 45202–4109
Phone: (513) 765–7000
reds.com

Colorado Rockies
Coors Field
2001 Blake Street
Denver, CO 80205–2000
Phone: (303) 292–0200
coloradorockies.com

Florida Marlins
Dolphin Stadium
2269 Dan Marino Boulevard
Miami, FL 33056
Phone: (305) 626–7400
marlins.com
marlinsbeisbol.com

Houston Astros
Minute Maid Park
501 Crawford Street
Houston, TX 77002
Phone: (713) 259–8000
astros.com
astrosdehouston.com

Los Angeles Dodgers
Dodger Stadium
1000 Elysian Park Avenue
Los Angeles, CA 90012–1199
Phone: (323) 224–1500
dodgers.com
losdodgers.com

Milwaukee Brewers
Miller Park
One Brewers Way
Milwaukee, WI 53214
Phone: (414) 902–4400
brewers.com

New York Mets
Citi Field
Flushing, NY 11368
Phone: (718) 507–6387
mets.com
losmets.com

Philadelphia Phillies
Citizens Bank Park
One Citizens Bank Way
Philadelphia, PA 19148
Phone: (215) 463–6000
phillies.com

Pittsburgh Pirates
PNC Park
115 Federal Street
Pittsburgh, PA 15212
Phone: (412) 323–5000
pirates.com

San Diego Padres
PETCO Park
100 Park Boulevard
San Diego, CA 92101
Phone: (619) 795–5000
padres.com
padresbeisbol.com

San Francisco Giants
AT&T Park
24 Willie Mays Plaza
San Francisco, CA 94107
Phone: (415) 972–2000
sfgiants.com
sfgigantes.com

St. Louis Cardinals
Busch Stadium
700 Clark Street
St. Louis, MO 63102
Phone: (314) 345–9600
stlcardinals.com

Washington Nationals
Nationals Park
1500 South Capitol Street, SE
Washington, DC 20003–1507
Phone: (202) 349–0400
nationals.com
losnacionales.com

American League

Baltimore Orioles
Oriole Park
333 West Camden Street
Baltimore, MD 21201
Phone: (410) 685–9800
orioles.com

Boston Red Sox
Fenway Park
4 Yawkey Way
Boston, MA 02215
Phone: (617) 267–9440
redsox.com

Chicago White Sox
U.S. Cellular Field
333 West 35th Street
Chicago, IL 60616
Phone: (312) 674–1000
whitesox.com
loswhitesox.com

Cleveland Indians
Progressive Field
2401 Ontario Street
Cleveland, OH 44115
Phone: (216) 420–4200
indians.com

Detroit Tigers
Comerica Park
2100 Woodward Avenue
Detroit, MI 48201
Phone: (313) 471–2000
tigers.com

Kansas City Royals
Kauffman Stadium
One Royal Way
Kansas City, MO 64129
Phone: (816) 921–8000
royals.com
losroyals.com

Los Angeles Angels
Angel Stadium
2000 Gene Autry Way
Anaheim, CA 92806
Phone: (714) 940–2000
angelsbaseball.com
angelsbeisbol.com

Minnesota Twins
The Metrodome
4 Kirby Puckett Place
Minneapolis, MN 55415
Phone: (612) 375–1366
twinsbaseball.com

New York Yankees
Yankee Stadium
One East 161st Street
Bronx, NY 10451
Phone: (718) 293–4300
yankees.com
yankeesbeisbol.com

Oakland Athletics
Oakland-Alameda County Coliseum
7000 Coliseum Way
Oakland, CA 94621
Phone: (510) 638–4900
oaklandathletics.com
losatleticos.com

Seattle Mariners
Safeco Field
P.O. Box 4100
Seattle, WA 98104
Phone: (206) 346–4000
Mariners.com
losmarineros.com

Tampa Bay Rays
Tropicana Field
One Tropicana Drive
St. Petersburg, FL 33705
Phone: (727) 825–3137
raysbaseball.com
raysbeisbol.com

Texas Rangers
Rangers Ballpark in Arlington
1000 Ballpark Way
Arlington, TX 76011
Phone: (817) 273–5222
texasrangers.com

Toronto Blue Jays
Rogers Centre
1 Blue Jays Way, Suite 3200
Toronto, Ontario, Canada M5V1J1
Phone: (416) 341–1000
bluejays.com

GLOSSARY OF COMMON SCOUTING TERMS

Arm speed: Referred to in connection with a pitcher's velocity. That is, if a pitcher is to have good speed on a pitch, he must whip his arm with above-average arm speed. Weak or slow speed invariably means that the pitcher doesn't throw very hard.

Breaking pitch: Anything from a curveball to a slider to a split-finger fastball.

Crow hop: A little skip-step that in infielder makes when he has fielded a ball cleanly and has time to make a strong throw to first. The "crow hop" gives the infielder a chance to set his feet straight before throwing.

Free agent draft: Held the first week of June for eligible players, this is major league baseball's system for replenishing its talent pool in the minor leagues. Eligibility rules are a bit tricky and change occasionally; if you aren't sure whether you are eligible, review the Appendix or check with a local scout in your area.

Gamer: Some ballplayers actually look more like prospects in a real game than in a tryout or pre-game workout. These kids are sometimes referred to by scouts as "gamers," or players who tend to bring out their potential during the heat of competition.

Going (went) away: A local ballplayer who has signed and gotten the chance to "go away" to play pro ball.

Good athletic body: Description of a ballplayer who has excellent physique and is well coordinated. Scouts feel more assured signing ballplayers who are obviously good athletes as well as good baseball players.

Good baseball instincts: Instincts usually develop only after a youngster has played lots of sandlot, high school, college, and other amateur ball. Scouts look for a ballplayer's "instincts" in running the bases, choosing which base to throw to during a play, and anticipating what might happen next in a game. A player with good instincts makes good decisions as he plays.

Good jump on the pitcher: Basestealers study a pitcher's move to the plate in order to anticipate the pitch and get a good jump.

Good mechanics: Usually refers to a pitcher's wind-up and form. Scouts like to see quick, easy, fluid motion. The fewer the moving parts, the less chance of that youngster ever developing an arm problem.

Incentive clause: Some ballclubs put such a clause in a player's initial contract stipulating that he will be rewarded with a specific bonus if he makes it to AA, AAA, or the major leagues. The amount can vary from a few hundred dollars to a few thousand, or more.

Instructional league: At the end of each minor league season (usually around Labor Day), each major league office sends its top prospects to the instructional league to workout under tutelage. This special "season" runs from mid-September to early November. Being invited to the instructional league is considered a great honor by most minor leaguers, as it means that they are seen as bona fide major league prospects.

Just a thrower: A pitcher who throws hard, but with little finesse or accuracy. Throwers usually have enough velocity to get by, but need to learn the finer points of pitching as they mature.

Makes things happen: A ballplayer who makes things happen is a welcome sight to a scout—he's the kid who starts a rally with an unexpected bunt, takes the extra base when nobody expects him to, or makes that hustling play in the field. An intangible quality, and a real plus.

Minor league salary: Typically around $1,000 a month for a five-month season in Class A ball, plus a modest meal allowance for road games. Minor leaguers are not paid during spring training, though accommodations during that time are generally covered by the club.

Movement: A pitch with good movement means the ball is tailing in, tailing out, moving up, or moving down.

Needs a third pitch: Most amateur pitchers have two pitches: the fastball and the curve. That is usually sufficient for amateur ball, but in the professional ranks, good hitters quickly learn to look for either of these pitches. Scouts will say that a youngster needs a third pitch, such as a slider or a change-up, so he'll have more luck keeping professional batters off balance.

O.B. (organized baseball): An older term referring to professional baseball or the minor leagues. These days, it means a team "affiliated" with a major league organization.

Organizational player: Sometimes a scout signs a marginal prospect because the organization happens to need an extra player in that position that season. This player, nonetheless a professional, is called an "organizational player" or O.P. because he has been selected to fill a role or slot rather than to be a major league prospect.

Out pitch: Not necessarily a strikeout pitch, but one thrown to pull the batter off-stride, in the hopes of his hitting a ground ball, pop-up, or fly out. The strikeout, of course, is just an added bonus. All professional pitchers have an out pitch that they save to use on a hitter at just the right time.

Patient hitter: A hitter who rarely swings at the first pitch, but waits the pitcher out, allowing several pitches to pass before swinging.

Quick bat: A hitter with a quick bat can wait on a pitch until the very last second and then unleash a powerful stroke. Ballplayers with quick bats are usually good hitting prospects.

Quick feet: Infielders with quick feet are able to adapt to bad hops or throws and other unexpected events during the course of a play and still keep their balance. One doesn't have to be fast to have quick feet: The term refers more to anticipation and balance than speed. It's another desirable trait scouts look for.

Quick hands: A term usually applied to an infielder or catcher, meaning an ability to adjust rapidly with one's hands to an unexpected bad hop or close play. A shortstop or second baseman with quick hands has the ability to take a tough-to-handle grounder and transform it into a routine out.

Quick release: A catcher with a quick release doesn't take much time receiving the pitch and firing the ball to second base on an attempted steal. A youngster can make up for a fair arm if he's accurate and has a quick release to second. Outfielders can be termed as having a quick release after catching fly outs.

Range: Refers to a defensive player's ability to cover a lot of ground. However, one's range means coverage in four different directions—to the left, to the right, frontward, and backward. Having excellent range is a key trait that scouts look for in a prospect.

Signing bonus: Different from an incentive clause, a signing bonus is a cash payment made to a prospect, drafted or undrafted, just for signing his name to the professional contract. The bonus normally is given without any requirements for performance.

Singles hitter: Scouts don't use the term negatively as is sometimes thought. Rather, a solid singles hitter is often regarded as a top prospect.

Sleeper: A potential pro player who was uncovered late in his career or passed over by most clubs and then "blossomed" when given a chance. Many sleepers are found at small schools or on the sandlots.

Slow bat: Hitters who tend to get jammed on pitches or loft the ball to the opposite field are sometimes labeled as having a slow bat. The usual feeling among scouts is that if a hitter can't get around on amateur pitching, he'll have even greater problems against major league pitchers.

Slow to the plate: Scouts carefully watch how fast a pitcher delivers to the plate with men on base. A hurler with a big leg kick is invariably slow to the plate, which allows baserunners to get big jumps for stealing.

Soft hands: Used primarily to describe infielders and catchers; refers to the ability to receive the ball with little effort and a sense of smoothness and grace. A player with soft hands has "give" in his catching motion as opposed to one with "iron" hands.

Some pop in his bat: A player with this ability usually has demonstrated, on occasion, that he can hit the ball with power and for distance.

Suspect: A ballplayer who has all the tools he needs to be a professional player is called a prospect. A ballplayer whose professional potential is questionable is labeled by scouts as a "suspect."

Table-setter: Usually the first two men in the lineup, the main job of these players is to get on base—to be the table-setters for the big RBI hitters batting behind them.

Upper-cutter: Some youngsters like to think of themselves as home run hitters and have therefore adopted swings in which they "uppercut" like Jim Thome or Ryan Howard. However, scouts realize that people like Thome and Howard are well over 6 feet tall, extremely strong, and very rare types of players; in reality, the typical professional hitter doesn't uppercut, but actually swings down on the pitch to hit line drives and hard grounders.

U.R. (unconditional release): Given to a professional player when the front office has decided his services are no longer required. After being released, a player can negotiate as a free agent with any other club interested in him.

Velocity: The raw speed of a pitch, which can be accurately clocked by a radar gun. Velocity does not refer to control, movement, or effectiveness.

Winter ball: Different from the instructional league. Some ballplayers, in hopes of making money from baseball all year round, head south to the Caribbean professional leagues during the winter months to stay in shape and make extra cash. Usually only ballplayers of major league of AAA caliber can find winter ball employment.

ACKNOWLEDGMENTS

First and foremost, I would like to thank the team at Skyhorse Publishing for giving us the chance to update and revise this book and make it available to an entire new generation of aspiring ballplayers. Mark Weinstein has been a fan of the book for a long time, and we were delighted to have him serve as the editor of this new edition.

In addition, we are most appreciative of the sales and marketing efforts of Bill Wolfsthal and Skyhorse's publisher, Tony Lyons. It has been a pleasure working with them as well.

This book would not have happened if it weren't for all the wonderful research and editing that Anita Tsuchiya of Sabaku Writing Services, Inc. offered. Anita was responsible for rounding up tons of great stories about players whose stories are peppered throughout the pages. Without those stories this book would not have come to life.

Thank you also to my dad, Rick Wolff, and to Al Goldis, who both wrote the two previous editions of this book. Your insights and experience, of course, created the strong foundation for this new edition, and your original message of inspiration and perspiration explain why the message of this book continues to be so popular twenty years after first being published

John Wolff
December 2008

ABOUT THE AUTHORS

Al Goldis has spent more than four decades as a major league scout, having worked in the front offices of the Cincinnati Reds, Baltimore Orioles, Anaheim Angels, Chicago White Sox, Chicago Cubs, and New York Mets organizations. In those 40-plus years he has seen and signed some of the game's greatest talents. As the scouting director of the Chicago White Sox in the late 1980s, Goldis spearheaded the amateur drafts that brought future All-Stars Frank Thomas, Robin Ventura, and Jack McDowell into the Sox organization. In 2009, Goldis was inducted into the Professional Baseball Scouts Hall of Fame.

John Wolff was drafted as a shortstop by the Chicago White Sox in 2005 after his junior year at Harvard University. He played just under three seasons in the minors and spent time with the Chicago White Sox, New York Mets, and in three Independent Leagues (Frontier League, Can-Am League, and the Atlantic League). He is the author of *Harvard Boys*, a detailed account of his first year in professional baseball. He is also the founder of eFieldHouse.com, an exclusive online community for professional athletes. John currently resides in New York City where he attends Columbia University's School of Business.